KT-370-176

I SHALL NOT HATE

'I met Dr. Abuelaish just a few days after the loss of his three daughters . . . We faced each other as we were about to shake hands. And then, without much thought, we held each other in a warm embrace . . . It is so rare, I thought, in this debilitating and devastating area we inhabit, to meet a person like him . . . a man who despite his own losses . . . continues his belief in humanity and its potential for good, despite all . . . Through his eyes I could see another way, a way the two nations could treat each other. A way that could extract what is good, special, and humane in both of them. I could see an alternative that could light up the great similarity of both peoples, one that gets denied and put down time and time again. This option, now so scorned and held in such contempt, suddenly sprang to life, embodied in the man I was watching.'

David Grossman

I SHALL NOT HATE

A GAZA DOCTOR'S JOURNEY
ON THE ROAD TO PEACE
AND HUMAN DIGNITY

IZZELDIN ABUELAISH

BLOOMSBURY
LONDON • BERLIN • NEW YORK • SYDNEY

First published in Great Britain 2011

Copyright © 2010, 2011 by Izzeldin Abuelaish
Foreword copyright © 2010 by Marek Glezerman

Originally published in Canada by Random House Canada in 2010

The moral right of the author has been asserted
No part of this book may be used or reproduced in any manner whatsoever without written permission from the Publisher except in the
case of brief quotations embodied in critical articles or reviews

Maps on pages ix and 64 by Ortelius Design. All other images courtesy of the author

Bloomsbury Publishing Plc
50 Bedford Square
London, WC1B 3DP

www.bloomsbury.com

Bloomsbury Publishing, London, Berlin, New York and Sydney
A CIP catalogue record for this book is available from the British Library

ISBN 978 1 4088 1367 6 (hardback edition)
ISBN 978 1 4088 1414 7 (trade paperback edition)

10 9 8 7

Typeset by Hewer Text UK Ltd, Edinburgh
Printed in Great Britain by Clays Ltd, St Ives plc

MIX
Paper from
responsible sources
FSC® C018072
FSC
www.fsc.org

To the memory of my parents—
my mother, Dalal, and my father, Mohammed.
To the memory of my wife, Nadia,
my daughters Bessan, Mayar, and Aya,
and my niece Noor.
To children everywhere.
Their only weapons are love and hope . . .

CONTENTS

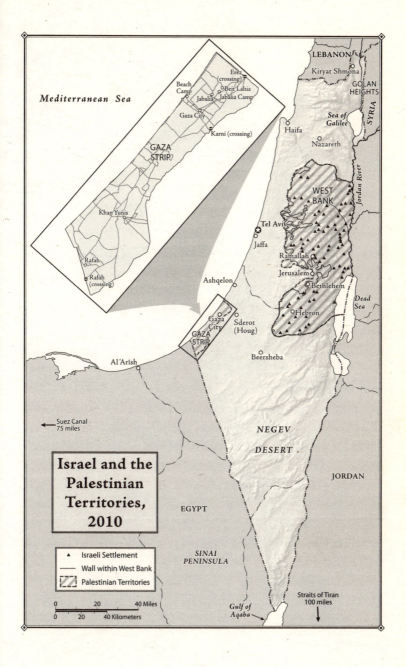

Mediterranean Sea

LEBANON
Kiryat Shmona

GOLAN
HEIGHTS

Sea of Galilee

SYRIA

Haifa

Nazareth

Erez (crossing)
Beit Lahia
Beach Camp
Jabalia
Jabalia Camp
Gaza City

GAZA STRIP

Karni (crossing)

WEST BANK

Jordan River

Tel Aviv

Jaffa

Ramallah

Khan Yunis

Jerusalem

Bethlehem

Dead Sea

Rafah

Rafah (crossing)

Ashqelon

Hebron

Gaza City

Sderot (Houg)

GAZA STRIP

Al'Arish

Beersheba

← Suez Canal
75 miles

NEGEV

DESERT

JORDAN

Israel and the
Palestinian
Territories,
2010

EGYPT

▲ Israeli Settlement

‒ ‒ ‒ Wall within West Bank

Palestinian Territories

*SINAI
PENINSULA*

0   20   40 Miles

0   20   40 Kilometers

Straits of Tiran
100 miles

*Gulf of
Aqaba*

Foreword

In the early nineties, when I was chair of the obstetrics and gynecology department at Soroka Medical Center in Beersheba,
Israel, Dr. Izzeldin Abuelaish contacted me for consultation
on patients he was treating in the Gaza Strip. From then on,
he used to bring his patients—mostly infertile couples—to me
after work, and I provided the consulting, usually free of charge.
In time, I came to know Izzeldin as a very dedicated physician
and empathetic human being and was impressed by his genuine
compassion for his patients. I also found the way he looked at
life and the world at large to be quite remarkable. Making the
trip from Gaza to Soroka hospital isn't easy. You never know
whether the border will be closed and if you will be able to get
back again. Given that he and his fellow Gazans experience
these frustrations on a daily basis, I found it extraordinary that
Izzeldin never generalized his complaints. I never heard him
condemn the injustices he suffered in general but only in specific,
very focused ways. This attitude is also reflected in his optimistic
outlook on life: he seems devoid of any existential pessimism or
hopelessness. He never dwells on "what could have been done
in the past," but rather on what can be done in the future. He is
forward-looking and full of hope, which isn't easy in this world
and is particularly hard in his world.

Another of Izzeldin's impressive character traits is his eager-
ness to improve his knowledge. He's always pushed for more

training and is never tired of learning and developing his skills. When I met him, he'd done obstetrics and gynecology in Saudi Arabia but he was dreaming of a formal residency in Israel. I regarded it as a great challenge to make him the first Palestinian physician to complete one. Residency programs in Israel are very intense and of high quality. Considering all the difficulties he faced living in Gaza, the question was not whether he was qualified for such a position but whether he would ever be able to make it work, since he never knew whether he'd be able to cross the border to fulfill the duties that awaited him here.

In 1995, at about the time I moved on to a chairmanship at another hospital, Izzeldin was admitted to the residency program in obstetrics and gynecology at Soroka Medical Center. It was an individually designed residency, not aimed at board exams but at completion of the curriculum. He completed it against all odds—all the different departments and rotations, troublesome border crossings, language barriers, and problems with schedules. For instance, if you don't show up, someone else has to pitch in for you on short notice, and nobody likes to do that. Depending on what was happening at the border, there were times when Izzeldin, along with all other Palestinians from Gaza, was not allowed to enter Israel. Sometimes after night shifts when the border was closed, he couldn't get back home to his family in Gaza. But he never called it quits. He completed the six-year program, he acquired full command of the Hebrew language, and he became a skilled gynecologist and obstetrician.

Izzeldin has every reason to be frustrated, disappointed, and offended by the environment he's lived in, but he is not. Despite everything he has seen and gone through, his belief in coexistence and in the peace process between Palestinians and Jews remains unshaken. He doesn't view Israel as a monolithic entity where everyone is the same. He knows many Israelis; some have become his friends. He knows many Israelis who don't dismiss all Palestinians as terrorists, and he knows many Palestinians who likewise do not look at all Israelis as right-wing occupiers. He believes that we are two peoples who want to live in peace and are fed up with war and bloodshed. In earlier times, ordinary people on both sides were more militant and the governments were perhaps more inclined to search for a solution. He believes that the situation is the reverse today: from the grass roots up, Palestinians and Israelis want to live in peace, to lead decent lives, to have roofs over their heads and safety for their children. It's largely the leaders in both camps who continue to fight the unfinished battles of yesterday.

Over the years, we've kept in touch. I see him at conferences, and of course we also have discussions about the conflict in the Middle East and about the chances for reconciliation. Both of us are optimists at heart. Neither of us believes that the ideological obstacles that prevent us from finding common ground for a decent future are insurmountable. When our leaders discuss peace now, they speak mainly about the future geographic borders between Israel and the emerging Palestinian state. The conflict has become a quarrel about real estate. And this can, must, and will be resolved one day. Of course, this is an oversimplification. There is no denying that many fanatics on both sides keep doing everything they can to advance their respective extremist visions. But they are the minority. Our true tragedy is that almost everybody knows what the outcome will be, yet too few are willing to admit it and act accordingly: two states living side by side, Jerusalem with a special status, the symbolic return of a few thousand refugees, and compensation for the ones who don't go back. The tragedy is the relentless march of follies in the opposite direction from this outcome, and all the Jewish and Arab casualties on that path. When people ask if my optimism results from idealism or realism, I have to say it's a mix of the two. You have to be realistic even if you're an idealist. And you have to be idealistic in order to cope with the reality here. If you judged our lives only by what happened yesterday or today, you'd never be able to lift your head and look to the future. If, on the other hand, you only look ahead, you'll stumble and walk in circles.

Izzeldin is realistic. He knows it's no rose garden we live in. But he strongly believes that medicine can bridge the divide between our peoples. Medicine and science know no boundaries or frontiers, nor should they. When I do research on a specific topic, I read publications and refer to data produced everywhere in the world—Japan, Syria, France, the United States. All that matters is the quality of the report, not where the authors come from. At international congresses we meet colleagues from all over the world, sometimes from countries that have no diplomatic relations with us or with each other. When I speak at scientific meetings, Arabs don't walk out the way they sometimes do at the United Nations. If I talk about medicine and science with a colleague whose country has no diplomatic relationship with Israel, we talk as professionals— although we may easily slip onto the personal level over coffee afterward. Accepting differing points of view is possible if you know each other.

Izzeldin visited our home a few weeks before the Israel Defense Forces began the bombardment of Gaza, and later we talked on the phone as the shells were falling. I asked him how he was handling his life under this bombing, living under constant curfew with his children at home. He said, "Like everyone else, we are all sleeping in the same room. We put some children against one wall and some against another wall so if we're hit we won't all be wiped out." On January 16, 2009, three of his girls were on the wrong wall. After this tragedy, who would have blamed him if he had been taken over by revenge and contempt?

A small group of influential Israelis asked for a formal investigation into the attack on Izzeldin's house, and the Ministry of Defense responded by stalling and evasion. Currently an increasing number of Israeli voices, including parliament members, are making the same demand on an even larger scale, but there is still no formal and independent Israeli investigation going on. What the Israeli authorities have come out with so far isn't sufficient. If a formal investigation comes to the conclusion that a huge mistake has been made, as it seems it has, the army should admit it in a straightforward and candid way—and apologize and take responsibility.

All of Izzeldin's remarkable energy could have been turned into hate, but he didn't take that path. Typically, he directed his energy toward a better place, which he summarized in a simple yet remarkable sentence: "If I could know that my daughters were the last sacrifice on the road to peace between Palestinians and Israelis, then I could accept it."

Izzeldin struggles for what he deeply believes in. He is dedicated to improving the environment he lives in by his own means, which is medicine. Albert Schweitzer, for example, may not have been the most acclaimed physician of his time, but through medicine he alerted the world to the suffering of Africans. He forced people to look at the African continent from a different angle and to understand what suffering is and what privileged people should do for the underprivileged. I strongly believe Schweitzer's major contribution to medicine was not so much by helping thousands of Africans as by awakening us to fellow human beings who were less privileged. Florence Nightingale is another example. She devoted her life to nursing and to improving medical care for the poor, and she demonstrated what the humanitarian role of medicine is. She showed that caring comes before curing.

I believe that Izzeldin has shown so much passion and compassion and dedication to bettering the human condition that this alone already makes him an extraordinary physician. But he transcends medicine. For Izzeldin, medicine is the tool to help people better understand the problems of one another, to better communicate, to help us live together. The many women he has treated or delivered at Soroka, his many Israeli colleagues with whom he has shared stressful situations in a busy clinical setup, who have pitched in for him and for whom he has covered on other occasions, his superiors and peers—all have encountered in Izzeldin a Palestinian doctor from the Jabalia refugee camp who treats his patients with professionalism and compassion, who is an equal among equals, and who has become a friend. The Palestinian patients who come to Soroka have encountered Israeli doctors and nurses who treat them with compassion, according to their medical condition and not their origin. This is how medicine bridges the divide between people.

About ten years ago, Izzeldin was going to a medical conference in Cyprus. He left the Gaza Strip and got to the airport, but the authorities wouldn't let him board his plane for security reasons. So he missed the flight. He only had a one-day travel permit, there wasn't another flight until the next day, and he couldn't stay at the airport. He was caught in a no-man's-land. Most people I know would have been furious. He called me, and I called some people and made arrangements for him to catch the plane the next day. He came to our house to stay overnight, and I expected to greet a very angry man. He was humiliated, but to my surprise he was angry only at a specific clerk at the airport, an individual person, not "the Israelis." That's Izzeldin— he never gets carried away into making wholesale judgments. He simply said, "That guy was not only inconsiderate, he was also misled. He behaved rudely because he did not understand."

Izzeldin doesn't generalize the way most of us do. For example, you may go on vacation to Italy and have a terrible cab-driver and a nasty hotel clerk and come home speaking badly of all Italians. Izzeldin would never react that way. He caught the plane the next day. He dealt with a clerk who wasn't looking for an excuse to punish an Arab, and he made it onto his flight.

Sometimes anger can be important, and people must be able to get angry. But Izzeldin directs his anger in a focused way, never spreading it wide and letting the anger overwhelm and distract him from where he should be going.

Under very tragic circumstances, Izzeldin has been pushed into the international spotlight. He has been interviewed by major newspapers, appeared on well-known TV shows, and met and talked to the leaders of the world. The amazing thing is that it hasn't changed him a bit.

Lately, I sometimes hear people say that he's too good to be true. Having lost his daughters, how can he still speak about peace and love and keep his Israeli friends? Some even wonder if he is taking advantage of this tragedy. But I have known him for many years, and I can attest that nothing could be further from the truth. His vision of coexistence is deep, strong, and consistent—unshaken even by a tragedy so enormous we have a hard time imagining how anyone could survive it. And still he moves on.

Izzeldin is now concentrating all his efforts on creating a foundation named after his dead daughters, aimed at promoting relationships between Jewish and Palestinian girls and contributing to their education, including the establishment of a school dedicated to this purpose. Wherever he goes, whomever he talks to these days, his main quest is finding ways to bridge the divide in our region. By now he has been able to touch many influential individuals with both his pain and his vision for the future, and I know he won't let go; if there is any single person who can make this happen, he is that person. I can only hope he succeeds.

—Dr. Marek Glezerman, chairman of the Hospital for Women and deputy director of Rabin Medical Center, Israel (adapted from an interview with Sally Armstrong)

Sand and Sky

It was as close to heaven and as far from hell as I could get that day, an isolated stretch of beach just two and a half miles from the misery of Gaza City, where waves roll up on the shore as if to wash away yesterday and leave a fresh start for tomorrow.

We probably looked like any other family at the beach— my two sons and six daughters, a few cousins and uncles and aunts—the kids frolicking in the water, writing their names in the sand, calling to each other over the onshore winds. But like most things in the Middle East, this picture-perfect gathering was not what it seemed. I'd brought the family to the beach to find some peace in the middle of our grief. It was December 12, 2008, just twelve short weeks since my wife, Nadia, had died from acute leukemia, leaving our eight children motherless, the youngest of them, our son Abdullah, only six years old. She'd been diagnosed and then died in only two weeks. Her death left us shocked, dazed, and wobbling with the sudden loss of the equilibrium she had always provided. I had to bring the family together, away from the noise and chaos of Jabalia City, where we lived, to find privacy for all of us to remember and to strengthen the ties that bind us one to the other.

The day was cool, the December sky whitewashed by a pale winter sun, the Mediterranean a pure azure blue. But even as I watched these sons and daughters of mine playing in the surf, looking like joyful children playing anywhere, I was apprehensive about our future and the future of our region. And even I did not imagine how our personal tragedy was about to multiply many times over. People were grumbling about impending military action. For several years, the Israelis had been bombing the smugglers' tunnels between the Gaza Strip and Egypt, but recently the attacks had become more frequent. Ever since the Israeli soldier Gilad Shalit had been captured by a group of Islamic militants in June 2006, a blockade had been put in place, presumably to punish the Palestinian people as a whole for the actions of a few. But now the blockade was even tighter, and the tunnels were the only way most items got into the Gaza Strip. Every time they had been bombed, they had been rebuilt, and then Israel would bomb them again. Adding to the isolation, the three crossings from Israel and Egypt into Gaza had been closed to the media for six months, a sign that the Israelis didn't want anyone to know what was going on. You could feel the tension in the air.

Most of the world has heard of the Gaza Strip. But few know what it's like to live here, blockaded and impoverished, year after year, decade after decade, watching while promises are broken and opportunities are lost. According to the United Nations, the Gaza Strip has the highest population density in the world. The majority of its approximately 1.5 million residents are Palestinian refugees, many of whom have been living in refugee camps for decades; it is estimated that 80 percent are living in poverty. Our schools are overcrowded, and there isn't enough money to pave the roads or supply the hospitals.

The eight refugee camps and the cities—Gaza City and Jabalia City—that make up Gaza are noisy, crowded, dirty. One refugee camp, the Beach Camp in western Gaza City, houses more than eighty-one thousand people in less than one half of a square mile. But still, if you listen hard enough, even in the camps you can hear the heartbeat of the Palestinian nation. People should understand that Palestinians don't live for themselves alone. They live for and support each other. What I do for myself and my children, I also do for my brothers and sisters and their children. My salary is for all of my family. We are a community.

The spirit of Gaza is in the cafés where narghile-smoking patrons discuss the latest political news; it's in the crowded alleyways where children play; in the markets where women shop then rush back to their families; in the words of the old men shuffling along the broken streets to meet their friends, fingering their worry beads and regretting the losses of the past.

At first glance you might think everyone is in a hurry—heads down, no eye contact as people move from place to place—but these are the gestures of angry people who have been coerced, neglected, and oppressed. Thick, unrelenting oppression touches every single aspect of life in Gaza, from the graffiti on the walls of the cities and towns to the unsmiling elderly, the unemployed young men crowding the streets, and the children—that December day, my own—seeking relief in play at the beach.

This is my Gaza: Israeli gunships on the horizon, helicopters overhead, the airless smugglers' tunnels into Egypt, UN relief trucks on the roadways, smashed buildings, and corroding infrastructure. There is never enough—not enough cooking oil, not enough fresh fruit or water. Never, ever enough. So easily do allegiances switch inside Gaza that it is sometimes hard to know who is in charge, whom to hold responsible: Israel, the international community, Fatah, Hamas, the gangs, the religious fundamentalists. Most blame the Israelis, the United States, history.

Gaza is a human time bomb in the process of imploding. All through 2008 there were warning signs that the world ignored. The election of Hamas in January 2006 increased the tension between Israelis and Palestinians, as did the sporadic firing of Qassam rockets into Israel and the sanctions imposed on Palestinians by the international community, as a result.

The rockets, homemade, most often missing their targets, spoke the language of desperation. They invited overreaction by the Israeli army and retaliatory rocket attacks from helicopter gunships that rained down death and destruction on Palestinians, often defenseless children. That in turn set the stage for more Qassam rockets—and the cycle kept repeating itself.

As a physician, I would describe this cycle of taunting and bullying as a form of self-destructive behavior that arises when a situation is viewed as hopeless. Everything is denied to us in Gaza. The response to each of our desires and needs is "No." No gas, no electricity, no exit visa. No to your children, no to life. Even the well-educated can't cope; there are more postgraduates and university graduates per capita here in Gaza than in most places on earth, but their socioeconomic life does not match their educational level because of poverty, closed borders, unemployment, and substandard housing. People cannot survive, cannot live a normal life, and as a result, extremism has been on the rise. It is human nature to seek revenge in the face of relentless suffering. You can't expect an unhealthy person to think logically. Almost everyone here has psychiatric problems of one type or another; everyone needs rehabilitation. But no help is available to ease the tension. This parasuicidal behavior—the launching of rockets and the suicide bombings—invites counterattacks by the Israelis and then revenge from the Gazans, which leads to an even more disproportionate response from the Israelis. And the vicious cycle continues.

More than half of the people in Gaza are under the age of eighteen; that's a lot of angry, disenfranchised young people. Teachers report behavior problems in schools—conduct that demonstrates outward frustration and a sense of helplessness in the face of war and violence. Violence against women has escalated in the last ten years, as it always does during conflict. Unemployment and the related feelings of futility and hopelessness create a breed of people who are ready to take action because they feel like outcasts—like they have nothing to lose, and worse, nothing to save.

They are trying to get the attention of the people outside our closed borders: those who make decisions about who is welcome and who is not. Their rallying cry is "Look over here, the level of suffering in this place has to stop." But how can Gazans attract the attention of the international community? Even humanitarian aid organizations depend on permission from Israel to enter and leave the Gaza Strip. There is a blatant abuse of power by people given the title of border patrol officer and a uniform, but who may not even understand the implications beyond a simple list of rules dictated by ego-driven leaders. They are disconnected from the common ground with others who are fellow human beings.

The acts of violence committed by the Palestinians are expressions of the frustration and rage of a people who feel impotent and hopeless. The primitive and cheap Qassam is actually the most expensive rocket in the world when you consider the consequences—the life-altering repercussions it has created on both sides of the divide and on the Palestinians in particular. The disproportionate reaction by the institutionalized military powers causes loss of innocent lives, demolishes houses and farms; nothing is spared, and nothing is sacred.

I've lived with this tension in varying degrees throughout my life, and have always done my utmost to succeed, despite the limits our circumstances have imposed on us. I was born in the Jabalia refugee camp in Gaza in 1955, the oldest of six brothers and three sisters, and our lives were never easy. But even as a child I always had hope for a better tomorrow. As a child, I knew that education was a privilege: something sacred and the key to many possibilities. I remember holding on tightly to my books the same as a mother cat would hold on to her newborn kittens, protecting my most valuable possessions with my life, in spite of any destruction that might have been going on around me. I loaned those treasures to my brothers and even some friends who were younger than I was. But before I did so, I let them know that they better take care of them as though they were their own most treasured possessions. I still have all those books today.

Through hard work, constant striving, and the rewards that come to a believer, I became a doctor. However, it wouldn't have been possible without the tremendous, untiring efforts of my parents and the rest of my family, who altruistically sacrificed everything, even though they had nothing, to support me throughout my time of studying. When I went to medical school in Cairo, they worried because I would be far away from them. Would I have enough to eat? Would I find our traditional foods? My favorite cookies; my favorite Palestinian spices; olives and olive oil? My mother would send these things with Gazans who came to visit Egypt. Sometimes I would receive packages of clothing, soap, apples, tea, coffee—all of which I needed, but also some of my favorite things. My family recognized my deep desire to make a better life for everyone and wanted to invest in me with very high hopes that I could help all of us. After medical school, I got a diploma in obstetrics and gynecology from the Ministry of Health in Saudi Arabia in collaboration with the Institute of Obstetrics and Gynecology at the University of London. Later, beginning in June 1997, I undertook a residency in obstetrics and gynecology at Soroka hospital in Israel, becoming the first Palestinian doctor to be on staff at an Israeli hospital. Then I studied fetal medicine and genetics at the V. Buzzi hospital in Milan, Italy, and the Erasme hospital in Brussels, Belgium, and became an infertility specialist. After that I realized that if I was going to make a larger difference for the Palestinian people, I needed management and policy-making skills, so I enrolled in a master's program in public health (health policy and management) at Harvard University. Then I worked as a senior researcher at the Gertner Institute in the Sheba hospital in Israel.

All of my adult life I have had one leg in Palestine and the other in Israel, an unusual stance in this region. Whether delivering babies, helping couples overcome infertility, or researching the effect of health care on poor populations versus rich ones, or the impact on populations with access to medical help versus populations without access, I have long felt that medicine can bridge the divide between people and that doctors can be messengers of peace.

I didn't arrive at this conclusion lightly. I was born in a refugee camp, grew up as a refugee, and have submitted myself on a weekly basis to the humiliation of checkpoints and the frustrations and endless delays that come with crossing into and out of Gaza. But I maintain that revenge and counter-revenge are suicidal, that mutual respect, equality, and coexistence are the only reasonable way forward, and I firmly believe that the vast majority of people who live in this region agree with me. Even though I could feel immense trouble coming our way in December 2008—an even broader threat to our sense of security than Nadia's death—these ideas were playing on my mind as I watched my children romping in the waves.

I chose that date, December 12, to bring them there because it followed hajj, one of the holiest days in the Islamic calendar; it was a time to reflect, to pray, to gather the family together. Hajj is the pilgrimage to Mecca that takes place between the seventh and twelfth days of the month of Dhu al-Hijjah in the Islamic calendar. This is the largest annual pilgrimage in the world; every able-bodied Muslim is required to make the trip at least once in his or her lifetime. Whether you go to Mecca or not, Waqfat Arafat is the Islamic observance day during hajj in which pilgrims pray for forgiveness and mercy. It's the first of the three days of Eid al-Adha that mark the end of hajj. In Mecca, pilgrims stay awake all night to pray on the hill of Arafat, the site where the prophet Muhammad delivered his last sermon. For the millions of Muslims, my family included, who do not go to Mecca each year, bowing to the Alkebla in the east, falling to your knees, and praying the prayers of the believer is sufficient. On the second day we mark the Feast of Sacrifice: the most important feast of Islam. It recalls Abraham's willingness to sacrifice his son in obedience to God and commemorates God's forgiveness. Everyone observes the day by wearing their finest clothing and going to the mosque for Eid prayers. Those who can afford to do so sacrifice their best domestic animals, such as a sheep or a cow, as a symbol of Abraham's sacrifice. We observed the prayer day in Jabalia Camp with our relatives and went to the cemetery at the camp to pray for Nadia. I'd bought a sheep and had it sacrificed, donated two thirds of the animal to the poor and needy, as is the custom, and had some of the rest of the animal made into kebabs for a barbecue at the beach to mark the final day of Eid.

We got up early the next morning, made sandwiches, and packed a picnic, and at seven A.M. we all climbed into my 1986 Subaru and set out.

Before we got to the beach, I had another treat for my children. In early December I'd bought a small olive grove, maybe a quarter of an acre in size and less than a third of a mile from the beach. It was like a little piece of Shangri-la, separated from the turmoil by a ten-foot-high fence, a place where we could be together, a place where maybe we could build a little house one day. I had kept it a secret until I could show them. As they tumbled out of the car, the kids were surprised and delighted with this unlikely piece of utopia on the outskirts of Gaza, with its olive trees, grapevines, fig and apricot trees. They explored every corner, marveled at the tidy rows of trees, and happily chased each other through the undergrowth until I reminded them that there was work to be done. We all dug into the task of tidying up this place, which was a little neglected and needed weeding. Even though they had known nothing but the crowded confines of the Gaza Strip for most of their lives, my children, the descendants of generations of farmers, seemed at home here.

After we had done enough work, we retreated to a small area of the grove bordered by a line of cinder blocks and shaded by an arbor of grapevines. We spread mats and made a small fire from the twigs and brush we had cleared from the olive trees, and sat in the shade of the vines eating our falafel sandwiches and talking about the events of our family life—the loss of my wife, their mother; a change so enormous we were still, three months later, reeling with grief while trying to come to terms with it.

I also needed to talk to them about another significant surprise. Recently I'd been offered a chance to work at the University of Toronto in Canada. Except for a brief stay in Saudi Arabia, where Bessan and Dalal were born, the family had never lived anywhere but Gaza. Moving to Toronto would be a monumental change, maybe even too overwhelming so soon after their mother died.

When I told them about the opportunity, Aya said, "I want to fly, Daddy." So I knew at least one of them was willing to leave everything behind—our home, the uncles and aunts, the cousins, the friends—and start over in a new country. Soon the others also agreed: together we would go to Canada, not forever, but for a while. The older girls, Bessan, 21, Dalal, 20, and Shatha, 17, would attend the University of Toronto; the younger children, Mayar, 15, Aya, 14, Mohammed, 13, Raffah, 10, and Abdullah, 6, would attend public school in Canada. There would be many challenges: attending classes in English, experiencing a Canadian winter, learning about a different culture. But we would also be out of the constant tension of Gaza; they'd be safe. These eight children had seemed to be adrift, even in our home, without their mother. This change would be good for them. Together, we would manage. I could see the excitement on their faces, and I felt a renewed sense of optimism for the first time in months. After the family discussion ended and we had cleared away our meal, the kids were eager to get to the beach. Fifteen of us, including the cousins and uncles, followed the rutted path up a small hill and through a meadow that led from the olive grove to the water. We walked all together, our group changing shape every few yards as one child ran ahead and two others stopped to examine an object on the path; the three girls walking together became five, arms linked. Eventually we all made it to the sand.

Despite the cool day, the children ran straight for the water, where they swam and splashed each other for hours, taking breaks to play in the sand. These children of mine—my offspring, my progeny—were the joy of my life, and they had meant the world to Nadia.

I had known Nadia's family before we were married in 1987, when she was twenty-four and I was thirty-two. It was an arranged marriage, as is the custom in our culture, but of the young women my family arranged for me to meet, Nadia seemed the most suitable. She was a quiet, intelligent woman who had studied to become a dental technician in Ramallah on the West Bank. Our families rejoiced at our union but were not as happy when we left Gaza almost immediately after our marriage for Saudi Arabia, where I had been working as a general practitioner. Nadia, too, felt the anxiety of dislocation. Though Bessan and Dalal were born there, Nadia never adjusted to living in Saudi Arabia, never felt that she belonged. The customs were different from the ones we were used to, and she keenly felt the separation from our extended family and wanted to return home, which we eventually did in 1991.

I traveled a lot after we settled again in Gaza (to Africa and Afghanistan for work and to Belgium and the United States for more medical training), but Nadia stayed at home with the children. We were a very traditional family, surrounded by my brothers and their families, my mother, who lived next door, and Nadia's mother and father, who lived nearby. Since I had to be away quite often, both Nadia and I felt the need to be close to other family members. She never complained about my frequent absences during the twenty-two years we were married. I could never have studied at Harvard or worked for the World Health Organization in Kabul, Afghanistan, or even done my obstetrics and gynecology residency in Israel, without the support she gave me.

It seemed surreal that she was gone. I watched my children and wondered what would become of them without their beloved mother. How does anyone come to terms with this sort of pain?

In the weeks since Nadia had died, Bessan, our firstborn, my oldest daughter, had assumed the role of mother as well as older sister. It was a particular relief this day to see her dashing into the sea, the surf soaking her jeans, her laughter carried away on the wind. She was a remarkable girl, my Bessan. She was on track to graduate from the Islamic University in Gaza at the end of the academic year with a business degree. She seemed to be able to handle everything: mothering the children, taking care of the house, and getting high marks at school. Since her mother had died, though, she began to see that exams were the easiest part, that there were other, harsher realities. It was a lot for a twenty-one-year-old to bear.

Dalal, my second-oldest daughter, was named after my mother. She was a second-year student at the same university as Bessan, where she was studying architectural engineering. She was a quiet, studious girl, shy like most of my daughters. Her architectural drawings were remarkable to me—a sign of the precision she demanded of herself.

Shatha was in her last year of high school and hoping to score the top marks in the class when they took their exams in June so she could fulfill her dream to become an engineer. The three girls were best friends and slept in the same room of our house in Jabalia City, a five-story building that my brothers and I had built. Each of us had a floor for his family; my children and I lived on the third floor. One brother lived apart from us in a separate house. When we constructed the apartment building, he said he wanted to be near but in his own place. So we built another house for him. The first floor of our house was reserved for our mother. (My sixth brother, Noor, had become caught up in the conflict of the region and has been missing for decades.)

Mayar and Aya, who were in grades nine and eight, were almost painfully shy. Sometimes they even asked one of their older sisters to speak to the others for them. But they were clever girls. Mayar looked the most like her mother, and she was the top math student in her school. She entered school competitions in Gaza and usually won. She wanted to be a doctor like me. She was the quietest of my six daughters, but she was not shy about describing the impact the strife in Gaza had on the people who live there. She once said, "When I grow up and become a mother, I want my kids to live in a reality where the word *rocket* is just another name for a space shuttle." Aya was never far from Mayar. She was a very active, beautiful child who smiled easily and laughed a lot when she was with her sisters. She wanted to be a journalist and was very determined in her own quiet way. If she couldn't get what she wanted from me— permission to go to visit a relative or to buy a new dress—she'd go to her mother and say, "We are the daughters of the doctor; you must give this to us." Aya loved language, excelled in Arabic literature. She was the poet in the family.

Raffah, my youngest daughter, with eyes as bright as stars, was an outgoing child, inquisitive, rambunctious, and gleeful. She was in grade four that year.

Mohammed, named after my father, was our first son, a young man of thirteen. He needed the guidance of a father, and I was worried about that because I was away four days a week, working at the Sheba hospital in Tel Aviv. He was to take the grade seven exams in June. His little brother, Abdullah, our second son, who was in the first grade, was the baby of the family. Watching him running to his sisters on the beach, kicking up the sand as he bounded over the dunes, I felt a special pain for this motherless boy: how much would he remember her?

That day they all sat for photos beside their names in the sand. Even Aya and Mayar smiled into the camera. When the tide came in and washed their names away, they wrote them again, farther up the beach. To me, this action was highly symbolic of their tenacious, determined nature, one that I recognized in myself. They had the ability to look for alternatives when situations seemed impossible; they were claiming this tiny piece of land as their own—because they believed that they belonged here and did not want to be erased. Wasn't this the same determination shown by Palestinians who'd had their land stripped from them and wanted to reclaim it? It reminded me that their mother's memory will never wash away, but that they could keep rewriting it in a different light. They rushed from playing in the surf and riding the waves to climbing into a boat that was moored on the beach, from building pyramids in the sand to racing back into the water; the camera click, click, clicking, recording the joy, the laughter in their faces, the bond they had with each other, their shared reality. As I watched the jubilance of my eight children, I thought, "Let them play, let them escape from their grief."

While they cavorted on the dunes, I drove back to Jabalia Camp to get the kebabs. There had been such a long line at the butcher early that morning that I'd decided to go to the beach and return for the meat once the children were settled. While driving, I thought about Nadia and the changes in our lives since she had died. At first I'd believed that I would have to stop the research work I was doing, since it required me to be in Tel Aviv from Monday to Thursday. But the children insisted that I continue. They said, "We'll take care of everything at home. Don't worry." It was the way Nadia had raised them. She was the example they were following. Nadia managed the house, the children, the extended family, everything, while I went away to study, to work, to try to make a better life for all of us. Sometimes I was away for three months. When I studied public health at Harvard from 2003 to 2004, I was gone for a year. But how could these children manage without a mother if their father was away more than half the time, even though they all told me that I needed to go on? This is why I was so happy they had agreed to move to Toronto; there we could all be together, with no border to cross every day.

And while we were in Canada, this place would be waiting for us. There is something eternal about olive, fig, and apricot trees, a piece of land that's near a beach where the sky meets the sea and the sand, where whitecaps break as waves roll up to the shore, where the surf rides high on the beach and the laughter of children soars on the wind.

The ringing of my cell phone brought me out of my reverie. It was Bessan, teasing me, saying, "Where is my father with the kebabs? Our stomachs are growling. We need food." I told her I was on my way and they should go back to the olive grove and get the hibachi started.

Later, we feasted on the kebabs, told more stories, and then returned to the beach for one last walk before the setting sun sent us home.

The strife of Gaza has been the backdrop of my children's whole lives, though I have tried my best to make sure that their experiences growing up would be less traumatic than my own. I remember clearly how grateful I was that day for the chance to get them out of there for a while, to fly them away with me before more trouble came our way.

My daughters had heard me speaking about coexistence throughout their lives. Three of them—Bessan, Dalal, and Shatha—had attended the Creativity for Peace camp in Santa Fe, New Mexico, which is run by Israeli and Palestinian coordinators. One of the coordinators, Anael Harpaz, told me she sees the youth of the region as the antidote that can counteract sixty years of acrimony. I wanted my daughters to meet Israeli girls and to spend time with them in a neutral setting in order to discover the ties that may bind and heal our mutual wounds. Getting the paperwork for the girls to leave Gaza for the United States was a monumental task, as Gazans cannot leave the Strip without permission from Israel. Nevertheless, this was an experience I desperately wanted my children to have: to see that people can live together, can find ways to cooperate and to make peace with each other. Bessan went to the camp twice. Dalal and Shatha had one visit each.

Bessan was the only one of my children to have met Israelis before going to the peace camp. In 2005, she joined a small group of five young women from both sides of the conflict for a road trip across America. Their leader, Debra Sugerman, took them in a van along with a cameraman to record their views on a multistate visit that was supposed to promote dialogue, create an understanding of each other's point of view, break down barriers between enemy cultures, and build bridges over the huge, complicated problems that existed between the two sides.

There were no easy answers during a journey that was layered with forgiveness, friendship, sorrow, and hope. Their conversations and activities were filmed for a documentary titled *Dear Mr. President*, and the girls hoped to meet President George W. Bush to enlist his support for the work they were doing.

For me, it was an example of what most families, most teenagers, and most scholars in the region want: to find a way through the chaos in order to live side by side. Some of the comments Bessan made in the film have stayed with me: "There is more than one way to solve a problem. To meet terrorism with terrorism or violence with violence doesn't solve anything." She also admitted that it's hard to forget what has happened here: the humiliation, the oppression of being basically imprisoned in Gaza and denied basic rights. That hurt of injustice lingers. "All problems can be solved by forgiving the past and looking toward the future, but for this problem it's hard to forget the past." Near the beginning of the documentary she says, "We think as enemies; we live on opposite sides and never meet. But I feel we are all the same. We are all human beings."

I have been straddling the line in the sand dividing Palestinians and Israelis for as long as I can remember, even as a fourteen-year-old when I worked for an Israeli farm family for the summer and discovered that they were as human as I was. As I watched the children on the beach that day, I saw the points in my life where I had crossed a line in the sand drawn by circumstances, by politics, by the ever-present enmity of two peoples. The abject poverty I lived in as a child, the opportunities I created through my performance at school, how the Six Day War altered my thinking—all of these and other crossings have shaped my life. From the time I was a very small boy I have been able to find the good chapter of the bad story, and that has always been the attitude I try to bring to the considerable obstacles that have challenged me. It is how I manage to move from one crossing to another. It seems to me that I gather strength from one to prepare for the next.

We stayed at the seaside until our shadows had become twenty-foot silhouettes on the sand. Then we went back to the olive grove, packed up our belongings, and the children bundled into the cars my brothers and I had driven that day, for the short journey home. Laughing about the day's events, mimicking and teasing each other as children do, the older ones looking out for the younger ones, they were bound together like rolls of twine in the backseats of the cars. As I drove, I listened to them chattering away, and I thought to myself, "We are getting there—they will be okay. Together, we can do this."

Exactly thirty-five days later, on January 16 at four forty-five P.M., an Israeli tank shell was fired into the girls' bedroom, followed swiftly by another. In seconds, my beloved Bessan, my sweet, shy Aya, and my clever and thoughtful Mayar were dead, and so was their cousin Noor. Shatha and her cousin Ghaida were gravely wounded. Shrapnel in his back felled my brother Nasser, but he survived.

The aftermath was carried live on Israeli television. Because the Israeli military had forbidden access to journalists and everyone wanted to know what was happening in Gaza, I had been doing daily interviews with Shlomi Eldar, the anchorman on Israel's Channel 10. I had been scheduled to do one that afternoon. Minutes after the attack occurred, I called him at the TV station; he was doing the live newscast, and he took the call on air.

The footage shot around the world and showed up on YouTube and in the blogosphere. Nomika Zion, an Israeli woman from Sderot, the town that is on the receiving end of Qassam rockets, said: "The Palestinian pain, which the majority of Israeli society doesn't want to see, had a voice and a face. The invisible became visible. For one moment it wasn't just the enemy—an enormous dark demon who is so easy and convenient to hate. There was one man, one story, one tragedy, and so much pain." This is what happened to me, to my daughters, to Gaza. This is my story.

TWO

Refugee Childhood

I cannot present my past without first describing the present and daily consequences of the recent history and tortured politics of Palestine, Israel, and the Middle East. Then, as you read back into the past, I hope you will carry with you an appreciation of the relentless absurdity of a system that does not allow humans to be human. When I lived in Gaza I was one of a very few Palestinians who had a permit to work in Israel. I would cross the border at Erez twice a week. I would go to work in Israel on Sunday unless the border was closed, in which case I would go on Monday and come home on Thursday. When people ask me what it's like, I wish they could come with me and find out for themselves.

Erez, located in the northern part of the Strip, about a ten-minute drive from my home, is the only crossing that serves as a pedestrian exit point for Gaza residents entering Israel. (The other crossings are Karni in the east, which, when it is open, is for cargo, and Rafah in the south, which goes to the Egyptian border and is usually closed.) It's hard for civilized people to believe what happens there: the humiliation, the fear, the physical difficulty, the oppression of knowing that, for no reason, you can be detained, turned back, that you may miss a crucial meeting, scare your family into thinking that perhaps, like thousands of others, you've been arrested. As an experience, crossing is never routine, often erratic, frightening, and exhausting. I was forced to take a taxi to the border instead of my own car because after the second intifada, Palestinians were not allowed into Israel driving their own cars. I did it twice a week every week for years.

On Thursdays, on the way home for the weekend from my hospital post in Israel, I would ask the taxi to first stop at a shopping center about three miles from the border. This is where the Palestinians lucky enough to be allowed to make the trip stock up on everything from brake fluid (for a car that's so old it needs new parts every few weeks) to foodstuffs (always in short supply in Gaza), Coca-Cola, plastic shoes (there are rarely any leather ones for sale), and flat-screen TVs. To us it feels like the Disney World of shopping before we return to the land that's closed, where everything is shut down, shut off, or shut out.

At the border, you proceed with luggage, briefcase, and sacks of purchases to the first checkpoint and join the lineup at the booth, where you present your passport and papers and submit to a search. The Israeli border officers may take every bag apart and search every pocket or simply give a cursory glance at your person and your goods. There is no way of knowing which treatment you'll receive and how long you'll be held up, so there is no way to predict when you'll arrive home. No means of transportation is allowed beyond the first checkpoint, so when you're cleared through, you have to walk with your luggage and whatever else you're carrying to the next stop: a sleek, stainless steel building that looks like a cross between an airline terminal and a prison, which was built in 2004 to screen for what Israel called terrorists. The walk is slightly uphill, a strain on anyone carrying heavy items. This billion-dollar building, with all its X-ray machines, monitoring equipment, special conveyor belts, and video cameras, was designed to process 20,000 to 25,000 people a day: workers who used to cross by the thousands to and from their jobs in Israel, journalists who came in by the dozens to file stories on Gaza, and aid workers from many humanitarian groups. Since almost no one is allowed to cross anymore, the place is often practically empty—except for scowling staff, medical evacuees from Gaza, and bored-looking humanitarian aid workers. It seems like a giant make-work project for Israeli guards on one side and Hamas loyalists on the other. (Hamas, an acronym which means "Islamic Resistance Movement," is a Palestinian organization that has governed the Gaza portion of the Palestinian Territories since winning a majority in the Palestinian Parliament election in January 2006.)

The brand-new outpatient clinic, supposedly the catch basin for medical emergencies coming from Gaza, is also in this building, and is just as empty. It is a state-of-the-art facility designed to treat thirty patients an hour, complete with an intensive care unit, paramedics, and ambulance services for transfer to Israeli hospitals. It stands like a monument to the intransigence that keeps people apart. This clinic was finally opened with great fanfare just two days after my daughters were killed. But everyone knew that Palestinians could not get treatment there since they wouldn't have permission to cross the border. It was closed shortly thereafter.

Inside the terminal, you're directed to the appropriate counter—women this way, men that way, foreigners here, nonforeigners there. More questions. Then, unless you get turned away, and many do, your papers are stamped and you're on your way through a series of confusing corridors that challenge anyone with a lot of baggage and leave a sensible person feeling there's trouble ahead. Which there usually is. Grumpy porters can carry your bags on their luggage carts for part of the way if you're willing to pay their fee, which changes by the hour. However, once out of the terminal, eventually you need to take the bags yourself—no one knows why—over approximately one mile of gravel, rock, dirt, and dust that leads to the Gaza side of the border. For equally inexplicable reasons, more porters appear about two hundred yards from the finish line and hoist your luggage. After paying them about ten shekels a bag (US$2.60), you're in Gaza.

Under the irritated gaze of Hamas guards, you haul your bags to the rickety table at the roadside and prepare for another grilling. Papers are searched. Luggage is opened and tossed about, then the contents are jammed back into the bags. A thrust of a chin sends you on your way again, still toting your luggage and, if necessary, holding the hands of any children who may have crossed with you, lest they stray into the path of the cars that speed up to the crossing.

The message of Erez is clear: don't live in Gaza, don't go to Gaza—no one will help you on either side of the most fractious and contested border on the planet. But it's the trip back across the border into Israel that really tells the tale of a population cordoned off and under siege. There are precisely twenty different checks at different gates and in separate locked rooms with whirring X-ray machines and cameras. Instructions, issued sometimes impersonally, sometimes with hostility, rarely reluctantly, include "Spread your legs, put your feet on the designated spots, raise your arms above your head." Most of the people who have crossed into Israel since the blockade began in 2006 are patients with special permission to exit for hospital appointments. Often they are carrying small children who can't be left behind, or they are struggling with illness or limping with the help of a cane or being pushed in a wheelchair. In other words, they are sick. Yet there at the checkpoint, they wait for hours, for no apparent reason; no explanation is given. The trek starts on the Gaza side with the glowering policemen of Hamas who leave you to bake in the sun while they process your papers. If you pass whatever test they're conducting but not telling you about, they nod toward the gate to no-man's-land. You trek first across an open field, then down a cement corridor, and finally into the stainless steel building, obeying red and green lights that tell you to stop or to go, passing into consecutive locked cubicles with more stop-and-go instructions. Disembodied voices bark from loudspeakers. There never seems to be a single person—Palestinian, Israeli, or foreign—who understands the whole procedure, so we all carry on trying to interpret signs and responding to demands, hoping for a speedy arrival at the other side.

My fellow travelers one day included old ladies with plastic bags of pita bread and Styrofoam containers of soup that they were bringing to relatives in Israeli hospitals, I presumed, to avoid the starvation patients invariably anticipate while they wait for treatment in places away from home. There were little children, some of them obviously suffering with illness, who also had to wait interminably for a light to flash green or a guard to mutter "Lakh," which means "Go."

At the other end of the terminal building that day, my suitcase was selected for special scrutiny. It had already been opened and X-rayed at least twice during this crossing. I opened the suitcase again with the patience I had cultivated over the years to reveal that it was stuffed with children's books for the Palestinian kids who were patients at the hospital where I worked. The security guard went through every one of the two-hundred-odd volumes. Pop-up giraffes and monkeys on springs jumped from the pages, surprising the guard, but she didn't crack a smile. A little boy next in line, clinging to his mother's hand, craned his neck to see and managed a grin as the images flashed by and animals leaped from the page.

The border staff at times will go to great lengths to explain that this is about security and the safety of all concerned and not meant as harassment. It's a story that's hard to swallow when you watch the clock ticking while a guard turns every single page of two hundred children's books and mutters something about the scanner not being available. When I first started crossing on a weekly basis, in the midnineties, all the soldiers were rude and arrogant, but with time and enough patience on my part they learned to accept my existence. Now, when I pass, they sometimes ask me for prescriptions for birth control pills for their girlfriends or for medical advice for themselves. Once a security agent held me up at the crossing, not to dispute my papers but to ask me a very personal question. She was getting married the following Saturday and her menstrual period was due two days before the wedding. She wondered if I had any advice for delaying the start of her menstruation. I did, and was happy to spend a few minutes giving her the information she needed.

It used to take an hour's drive over paved goat trails to get from Gaza to Jerusalem. Today it's a half-day journey if you're lucky—if you have an exit pass, if the border remains open rather than suddenly closing, if the bus arrives on time and the traffic isn't snarled, and if the security officers aren't giving lessons in patience. For Palestinians, crossing at Erez is a real lesson in tolerance and compromise, both of which are usually in short supply in Gaza and Israel.

Crossing into Egypt is yet another story. Let me share with you the details of travel for a Gazan. Unlike the luxury taken for granted by so many in this world who travel for enjoyment, entertainment, and fun, for Palestinians in general and Gazans in particular, traveling is only permitted for a purpose: to study, work, or for medical treatment abroad that is not available in Gaza. Crossing the border with Egypt at Rafah, the only exit and entry point for people from the Gaza Strip, is a journey filled with humiliation, suffering, frustration, and oppression. This suffering is a deliberate act perpetrated by other humans.

It starts in the offices of the interior ministry, where Gazans are required to register and give justification and proof of their need to travel. Patients must present medical reports and the physician referral for treatment abroad. Only patients who are severely or terminally ill with cancer or cardiac or other medical problems can seek treatment outside of Gaza. Gazans working outside Gaza have to prove that they have a work permit and a visa to the country that employs them. Students must submit proof of their student status from their university.

People are powerless to decide when they are to travel. They wait to learn that the border is open every two to five months for a period of one, two, three, or four days, for humanitarian reasons only, for example, to patients who have no treatment in Gaza, students studying in Egypt or other countries, and Palestinians who came to Gaza to visit but who are working in the Gulf, Europe, or Western countries.

Once it is announced that the next day the border will be open—it's always a sudden, unexpected announcement—everyone rushes to search for their names on the registration list. The lucky ones will find their names, along with which day they are assigned to cross, which bus they are to take, and when to be at the place where the buses are loaded. One bus can fit forty to fifty passengers. The buses have to leave in groups and are numbered from 1 to 20 or whatever the allowed number to cross is for that day.

It takes time for the buses to get going, given all the chaos and disorganization. Let me recount just one of my horror stories. I arrived at seven A.M., and our bus started out with about forty passengers. By the time we finally moved at eleven A.M., we had about sixty-five passengers on board, all of us, including women and children, squeezed in like sardines in a can. We then proceeded to another stop to collect still more passengers and to be checked yet again. It was summer and the bus was not air-conditioned, and we were sweating and suffocating. We were able to breathe again once the bus moved inside the Rafah border, where we disembarked and our passports were processed and stamped by the Palestinian side. Then we returned to our assigned bus. This alone took two to three hours. But we were not finished yet. The bus moved about two hundred yards to the Egyptian gate. There were a few buses waiting in line, and each took about an hour to empty its passengers on the Egyptian side of the border.

The people were worried as rumors began flying that the Egyptians were returning people and not allowing them in. The fears and suspicions were grounded. I saw the returning buses carrying about 50 percent of their passengers back across the border. What was happening?

It was now about four P.M., five hours since our departure that morning. We were now told that the border would be closed. What could we do? Were we going to be taken back to Gaza? Were we going to have to stay there overnight on the bus without anything to eat or drink? Women, children, old and young?

At nine P.M. we were informed that the border guards

would continue to work and allow the buses through. We all returned to the buses, everyone scrambling to be in the first bus for fear the border would be closed by the time the later ones arrived. I was in the second bus, which now held about eighty passengers with their bags. With great difficulty, the door was closed.

Once the Egyptian gate was opened, I felt as though it was the gate to paradise. An Egyptian police officer entered our bus to count the passengers and check our passports. We had to wait in the bus; we were not allowed to get off. At about eleven P.M. or midnight our bus was ordered to move, so we were allowed to get off and go to the passport section. We thought this was the end and that we would be allowed to get on with our business.

Traveling with me was a sixty-five-year-old neighbor whose wife was Egyptian, and they and their children had lived in Egypt after the Israeli occupation of 1967. As of the 1967 occupation, the rule was that if you were not counted in the census done by the Israelis, you were not eligible to stay in Gaza but could only come as a visitor and leave after a limited time. After the Oslo Accords were signed in August 1993, he had arrived in Gaza as a visitor and stayed with his brothers and sisters past the time he was allowed, but then applied for family reunion status, which had to be approved by the Israeli government. He remained in Gaza until 2008, when his family reunion status was approved. He was finally free to come and go between Gaza and Egypt after having been issued a Palestinian passport and ID; but this too had to be approved by the Israelis. He said he had coordinated things so that he would be allowed entry to Egypt even though he was not a patient, a student, or someone traveling with a visa; so he assumed that everything would be fine with him.

Now for the surprises. At the door of the bus stood an Egyptian security officer, reviewing the papers of each passenger one by one and classifying them. One was directed to the right, one to the left; this passenger here, this one there. What was this?

I showed him my passport and my visa, and he told me to go inside the building where the passports were processed.

When I entered the building to submit my passport to be signed, I saw hundreds of people waiting inside a big hall. I noticed my neighbor and asked him how things were going with him. He told me everything was fine and they were going to allow him into Egypt. Soon, though, I heard a commotion and looked around. I found my neighbor screaming as an Egyptian policeman asked him to bring his bags so that he could be returned to Gaza.

He wasn't the only one. Arriving patients had to be checked by Egyptian doctors to confirm that their proof was credible and valid. Some were sent back on the same bus that had brought them there. After all this, to be returned at one A.M. on the second day of travel suffering from exhaustion, oppression, frustration, and despair—it was a disaster.

Imagine yourself in this position. What would you do? What could you do? How would you behave? Do you think anyone in that position can think rationally? If he were to commit any sins, I think we would have to understand why.

My neighbor had no choice but to turn back and do as he was told. Others with visas to other countries were waiting to see what would happen to them. Some, who had been approved entry to Egypt, were taken in groups from the Rafah border to the airport and were allowed to stay there and book their tickets. I was one of the lucky ones who was approved to enter

Egypt and stay in Cairo and travel by myself outside of Egypt. I arrived at my hotel at about seven A.M. the next morning, after twenty-four hours of humiliation.

Getting back to my crossing of the Erez border into Israel, as I would drive away from the border crossing, I would see many signs of a past that can seemingly never be recaptured. Old stone huts and storage barns from Palestinian farms stand abandoned in the fields in nearby southern Israel like markers of a bygone era; gaping holes where windows used to be are jammed with encroaching weeds, the hearths inside empty, cold. These are the inanimate reminders of the old Palestine; the living ones spring from the ground in the form of the sabra plant. It's a cactuslike succulent that has been used for thousands of years as a hedge to mark the borders of Palestinian farmlands. The prickly exterior hides a sweet fruit; the rubbery leaves are beautiful in their way, each one unique, with protrusions like stubby toes. For sixty years the land has been bulldozed, reassigned, and developed as if to scrub out any vestige of the Palestinians who lived, worked, and thrived here. But the enduring sabra plant remains like an invincible sentry, silently sending the message "We were here, and there, and down by the river and over near those woods and across that field. This land is where we were."

Coincidentally, the plant's name in the Arabic language means "patience and tenacity." Like the roots of the stubborn sabra that have defied the shovel of deportation, the people of Gaza have had to dig in and seek survival.

My childhood was spent in the shadow of a promise: We'll go back soon. Maybe in two weeks, maybe a little longer. But eventually we'll leave this brutal place and go back to the land of our forefathers, where we belong.

The village where my father and his father and the fathers who came before them lived is called Houg. It's in the southern part of Israel, near Sderot. There were kibbutzim all around my family's land, the village cemetery was nearby, and sheep grazed as far as the eye could see. At least, that's what I learned as a child, as stories of our earlier times were repeated again and again. In the confines of our treeless, provisional refugee camp, I learned that my grandfather, Moustafa Abuelaish, was the village *mukhtar*, or head, and that our family had been large and rich, one of the most eminent families in south Palestine. The Abuelaishes were well known for their generosity. The name itself—Abuelaish—means that everyone who arrives is fed, a symbol of hospitality in a fertile land where wheat, corn, figs, and grapes grow, where sheep are raised for milk and cheese. *El Aish* means "bread." *Abu* is the one who gives bread, hospitality, and care to his guests.

In the refugee camp where I was born, my family told these stories of our old life so vividly that they played on inside my head as I was falling asleep throughout my childhood. But I never saw that place. We never went back. I was born seven years after my father walked away from his heritage. He wasn't chased out as others were after the division of Palestine and the creation of the Israeli state in 1948 and the beginning of what is called the Nakba (the "Catastrophe"). Nor was the family wounded as others were in massacres that were happening throughout the region. No, my paternal grandfather decided it would be wise for the whole extended family to leave—just for a little while, until the terrible tension settled down. It was important to him that the family keep its dignity and honor.

There was a lot to consider in that disruptive year of 1948, with rumors of massacres taking place not far from the family farm, frightening stories of people escaping from the killing fields after witnessing the slaughter of their neighbors. He didn't know whether the rumors were true, but for the sake of the safety of the family, he had to act.

Gaza was a short distance away from Houg; it was the closest safe place for the family to go and had been designated as a location for Palestinians. The other refuge, known as the West Bank and located on the Jordan River, was foreign to my family, unfamiliar. So they went to Gaza. But the music of our former life in Houg played like a theme song throughout my childhood. There was always the promise, always the message that we were the Abuelaish family—the ones who took care of others, who gave to guests, who belonged to the land. My father never gave up the ownership papers of his farm. Even today, though the land at Houg is known as the Sharon Farm and Ariel Sharon is listed as the owner, the deed and tax papers stay with me. I don't keep them in order to make a case to get the family land back in some international treaty, but because failing to acknowledge what went on when the land changed hands is like a missing piece of a puzzle that remains unfinished. I try to explain to my own children that Gaza wasn't always a war zone or a prison. Before 1948, Gaza had many incarnations, none of them entirely peaceful and almost all of them noteworthy. The earliest recorded reference to Gaza is in Egyptian texts and refers to Pharaoh Thutmose III's rule when Gaza was the main city of the Land of Canaan and the only overland route between Asia and Africa. Much of Gaza's history comes from ancient stories told in the Quran, the Bible, and the Torah. The Philistines arrived in Canaan around 1180 B.C.E., during the Iron Age, and made Gaza a famous seaport. The infamous Delilah of biblical fame was one of those Philistines, and Gaza was the place where she delivered Samson into bondage. Palestine derives its name from those Philistines who ruled the area at that time.

Today Gaza is a strip of land approximately twenty-five miles long. It is about four miles wide at its narrowest and almost nine miles at its widest. Israel controls everything—the air, the water, the land, the sea. The Palestinian American attorney Gregory Khalil said in 2005, "Israel still controls every person, every item of commerce, even every drop of water that enters or leaves the Gaza Strip. Its troops may not be there . . . but it still restricts the ability for the Palestinian Authority to exercise control." His judgment of the situation is shared by most human rights organizations.

Throughout history, Gaza has been eyed by outsiders who had conquest on their minds. Alexander the Great tried to rule it; the Israelite king David ruled for a while, as did the Egyptians, the Assyrians, the Babylonians, Persians, and Greeks. So did Napoleon, the Ottomans, and the British. It seems that every warrior king or eminent general who made it into the history books has taken a run at Gaza.

The historical event that shaped the existence of every Palestinian today is of course the Nakba of 1948. There had been talk about creating a Jewish state since the end of the First World War.

The British mandate in Palestine had been created by the League of Nations, and the British had been assigned the job of implementing the Balfour Declaration, which would establish Palestine as the national home of the Jewish people. The agreement, reached on November 2, 1917, is so important to the history that followed that I want to cite the whole document.

Foreign Office,
November 2nd, 1917.

Dear Lord Rothschild,

I have much pleasure in conveying to you, on behalf of His Majesty's government, the following declaration of sympathy with Jewish Zionist aspirations which has been submitted to, and approved by the Cabinet:

"His Majesty's Government view with favour the establishment in Palestine of a national home for the Jewish people, and will use their best endeavours to facilitate the achievement of this object, it being clearly understood that nothing shall be done which may prejudice the civil and religious rights of existing non-Jewish communities in Palestine, or the rights and political status enjoyed by Jews in any other country."

I should be grateful if you would bring this declaration to the knowledge of the Zionist Federation.

Your sincerely
Arthur James Balfour

The trouble began with those words. Jews were a minority in Palestine, outnumbered by Arab Christians and Muslims. All of the rights of all of the non-Jewish people in the region were prejudiced by their expulsion from their homes and farms. The British mandate in Palestine ended on May 14, 1948, the same day the Israelis announced their Declaration of Independence and the birth of the Jewish state. Gaza, according to the United Nations partition plan of 1947, was supposed to become part of an independent Arab state, but the terms were not acceptable to the Palestinian people, who were forced to walk away from their homeland. Nor was the plan acceptable to their Arab neighbors. So when Israel declared its independence, Egypt acted on behalf of the rest of the region and invaded from the south, triggering the 1948 Arab-Israeli War.

Since then, a string of well-known dates has marked our failure to coexist: the Sinai War of 1956, the Six Day War of 1967, the Yom Kippur War of 1973–74, the intifada of 1987, the second intifada of 2000. There have been endless accords and agreements and several different leaders: the Oslo Accords of 1993, the Palestinian Authority, which gave self-rule to Palestinians under the leadership of Yasser Arafat in 1994, the Palestinian parliamentary elections of 1996, and the rise of Hamas in 2006. In 1948 the Palestinians were accused of wanting to throw the Israelis into the sea. David Ben-Gurion, the founder of Israel, was asked at that time how he would deal with the Palestinians who lost their land and had been deported. He replied, "The old will die and the new generations will forget." But look at the situation today: no one threw the Israelis into the sea, and the Palestinians didn't forget. However, after six decades in which the largest harvest in the region has been misunderstanding and hate, it is fair to say that forgetting the past is not the only issue; we need to find ways to go forward together.

I was born on February 3, 1955, in the Gaza Strip, a refugee child, and I had three strikes against me right from the start: we were poor, my family had been dispossessed, and I was the son of the second wife. Let me explain. My father married his first cousin, and they had two sons when they lived on the family farm in the village of Houg. It was 1948 when he brought the family to Gaza to avoid the possibility of being deported. My mother, Dalal, was from another village called Demra, closer to the Erez Crossing. When my father and his family left Houg for Gaza, they walked north a few miles to Demra, and it was my mother's grandfather who invited the family to rest there. My father thought Dalal was beautiful, and she was divorced. He fell in love with her and left his first wife, Aisha. After he had settled in Jabalia Camp, he sent for my mother and they were married, though I'm not sure when—sometime around 1950. Aisha continued to live close to us, with my two half-brothers, and my father continued to support them financially.

It was unusual in those days to marry someone from another village, someone to whom you were not related, and so my mother was ostracized by the rest of the family. However, my paternal grandfather accepted her; it was the cousins and uncles and aunts who were nasty, never including my mother in family events, shunning her on the street. While I was growing up, the first wife and her two sons lived in one house and my eight siblings and I lived with our mother, the second wife, in another house about two hundred yards down the street. I thought that my father was divorced from his first wife, because he lived with us, but he wasn't; he was only separated, and that created a lot of problems because he left her stranded, although he supported her financially. Some believe that Islam allows men to marry one, two, three, even four wives, something I don't agree with, but still, something that is controlled by the needs and norms of the culture. So with a marriage that wasn't going well, it was acceptable to marry another wife and leave the first wife hanging, but not to divorce her; divorce was not an acceptable alternative to happiness.

No matter my father's opinion, his extended family obviously preferred his first wife, and we were treated like strangers, looked upon as the sons and daughters of the foreign woman. Even though we all lived in the same neighborhood, even though my father provided for both families, we were the ones who were punished. I remember the hurt we felt during the feast of Ramadan when my uncles and aunts would give gifts and money to the children of the first wife but nothing to my siblings or me. Those children had special clothes to wear; we did not. No one in the extended family came to mark feast days with us. We were made to feel different. While we loved our mother, this aspect of our childhood remains a source of sadness.

A lot of people I knew in the Jabalia refugee camp focused on what was lost. The camp in the Gaza Strip wasn't far from Houg—about a six-mile walk. So our past lives and family history lingered only a few hours away. My family hadn't carried much with them when they left in 1948, because they were certain they wouldn't be gone for long. Gaza wasn't a refugee camp yet, just a place designated for Palestinian people when the state of Israel came into being. But day by day it filled up with people who had no place else to go. In 1949, when the United Nations Relief and Works Agency for Palestine Refugees (UNRWA) in the Near East came to the area, the number of exiled Palestinians was growing exponentially as more regions of Palestine fell under the ownership of the new state of Israel. Ultimately, the agency designated eight refugee camps in Gaza, Jabalia being the largest. It was located in the northern part of the Gaza Strip, and after the Arab-Israeli War it housed thirty-five thousand refugees in about one half of a square mile. More than two hundred thousand live in Jabalia Camp today. My parents moved from one small shelter to another, still thinking it was just a matter of time before they would be able to return home. Yet slowly, over the decades, temporary displacement became permanent reality with the burgeoning of the spaces outside the camps, such as

Jabalia City and Gaza City. Even inside the camps, real estate traded hands and businesses waxed and waned with the times.

I remember my paternal grandfather holding court in the refugee camp. Everyone came to listen to Moustafa Abuelaish because of the position he had held in the village of Houg. I saw him as the rock, the man with the power, the leader who discussed the issues of the day. He was highly respected and set an example for all of his sons, brothers, and cousins, and even for my family, as he was the only one who came to see us regularly. I was only a youngster at the time, and children weren't allowed to sit with the older people; I knew mostly by the way others came to listen that what he had to say was important. He and his peers talked a lot about being displaced. I suppose that was natural for people who felt they had been forced from their homes. Your home is where you feel safe or at least grounded, whatever and wherever it is. To be pushed out of it is to be marked with the scar of expulsion for the rest of your life. Even now, six decades after my family became refugees in the Gaza Strip, knowing that our family land will never be ours again, I still suffer from this loss. However, I was never drawn in by the loss, nostalgia, and outrage my grandfather expressed. I learned instead to direct my attention to studying and surviving. I knew there was a better way, and even as a child, I set out to find it.

Like most Palestinian children, I didn't really have a childhood. Until I was ten, my family, which eventually numbered eleven (two parents, six boys—I was the eldest of them—and three girls), lived in one room that measured about ten feet by ten feet. There was no electricity, no running water; there were no toilets in the house. It was dirty. There was no privacy. We ate our meals from a single plate we shared. We had to wait in line to use the communal toilets and wait for water that was delivered by the United Nations. We were only allowed to fill our pots during certain hours of the day. We waited for trolleys to come by with kerosene or wood for us to buy to cook with. We were usually barefoot, flea-bitten, and hungry.

We all slept together on a huge mattress that was hoisted up against the wall by day and lowered at night—except for the baby. There was always a newborn, it seemed, who slept in the same basin my mother used to wash the dishes, scrub the kids with a loofah, and clean the house. When we were ready for bed, she'd wipe out the dish bucket and use it as a cradle for the baby to sleep in.

One night my brother Nasser was acting up, aggravating my mother. She reached out to slap him, but he got away from her and she leaped up to chase after him. He jumped into the dish bucket to escape her, landing on top of the baby. The baby, my sister, who was only a few weeks old, died. It's hard even to imagine a baby dying like that. I was five years old at the time and don't remember the exact sequence of events. My mother grabbed the baby; she was crying and screaming. Nasser escaped by running outside. I do remember that female babies were not valued; people saw it as a tragedy if a newborn wasn't a boy. It was the way the culture was at that time. The little baby girl, called Noor, was buried in the cemetery the next day, and we never spoke about the incident again. It's the worst memory I have of growing up. In an overcrowded refugee camp, people cling to hope by a thread that threatens to break at any moment.

I don't really know how my father bore it—the conditions we lived in—given that he had lived the first part of his life on the family farm where there was plenty of food and just as much pride. My father was thirty-five years old when I was born. He was of average height, but he was strong. He always wore the national Palestinian clothes and wrapped his head in a kaffiyeh, the rectangular piece of cloth draped over the head and held in place by a cord called an *ekal*, made famous by the Palestinian leader Yasser Arafat. My father was the second in his family, a hardworking and successful farmer, but in the camp he had to search for odd jobs that never paid enough to feed his first wife and two sons and all of us. I remember once he had a job as a guard at an orange grove. My mother would pack a lunch for him and give it to me to deliver. For me, this task was of enormous importance, and I swelled with pride each time my mother handed me his food, honored by the trust she had in me. But even at six I understood the angst he felt at being a provider who could barely sustain his family.

My mother was tall and pale-skinned, with a strong personality. Her courage and determination made her a great role model. Indeed she challenged everyone who crossed her path. It was my mother who had the character and tenacity that helped us cope with the changed circumstances of our lives, the deficiency, the want, and the incessant need. She would fight for us, protect us, and whenever it was possible, she did not hesitate to take over the economic lead from my father. She raised goats and pigeons in our small space. She got milk from the goats and eggs from the pigeons, enough for our table and something left over to sell at the market to make money. After I started my education, she'd come to the school to ask my teachers how I was doing. I didn't want her to come, would beg her not to embarrass me in front of my friends, who would all tease me, saying, "Your mama is here." But it didn't stop her. She wanted to know how I was doing, so she came to the school to ask.

I don't dwell much on that time, but I do remember how painful it was, before I got to go to school, to sit on the stoop outside our house and watch other children walk past on their way to kindergarten, dressed in their handsome uniforms. A uniform was something my family couldn't afford, so I couldn't go no matter how eager I was to learn. Remember, there were people living in Gaza long before the refugees arrived. Their lives were vastly different from ours, and although they didn't live in the camp, those children walked by our home every morning while I burned with jealousy and told anyone who would listen that it was unfair that only some children got to go to school. But the majority of the people we knew were in the same situation: too busy with survival to worry about coming up with the money for school fees or uniforms so they could send their children to kindergarten.

At last, in 1961, when I was six, I was able to go to the United Nations school in the camp. But even at that school, which was staffed by Palestinian teachers, the prizes went to the kids who were deemed to be the best dressed. Old habits die hard; this school may have been run by an international body, but local rules held firm. The teachers called it the "cleanliness prize," but we all knew it was for the kids with the nicest clothes. I was dressed in hand-me-downs that had been stitched and restitched so many times that there were more mended threads in my trousers than original ones. I thought the awards should have been given to the students who got the highest marks. It would be several years before the system changed and students with academic prowess came to the attention of the teachers. That would be my salvation.

My first morning in the United Nations school, I was apprehensive for more reasons than just first-day jitters. My mother had found a pair of overalls for me to wear, an item of clothing I'd never seen before. Like almost all of our clothes, the overalls were hand-me-downs donated by other people, even from other countries. I was worried because I could not figure out how I would get the overalls off if I had to go to the bathroom. I got through the day all right, and once I got home that night, I figured out how to get the overalls off and on again. But the memory has stuck with me to this day.

The overalls weren't my only concern. It turned out the school was already overcrowded. On that first day, some of the students, me included, were told we'd be attending a school that was farther from my home. The other kids who had been picked to move weren't my neighbors or my brothers, and I didn't want to go with them. But my parents weren't there, so there was no one to speak up for me, to insist I should stay in the school near where we lived and attend classes with my friends. I had no choice but to move to the other school. (What I could not have known was that a teacher at the new school, Ahmed Al Halaby, would become one of the most important mentors of my life. He treated me like a son. I learned from the experience that you shouldn't hate something you don't know, because it may turn out to be the bearer of your greatest good fortune.)

That first year at school, I had three different teachers. One sat on a chair and passed out textbooks for us to read, and another gave us music lessons, which I liked a lot. The third was a man who acted as though he'd discovered a student in me. He paid so much attention to me that by the end of the year he had thoroughly convinced me, a first grader, that I could learn anything I wanted to learn and become anything I wanted to become. He was an extraordinary man.

The school was crowded. We sat three to a desk with sixty kids in every class, but I could hardly wait to get there every morning. I loved being at school, enjoyed the challenge of learning new things, and when the teacher asked a question, my energy level shot up as I raised my hand to answer. New information was like a gift to me. This was the place where I found out what I could do. By the age of seven, as the eldest boy, I was expected to help the family with money—earn a little here, a little there, to plug this hole or that hole. For example, the United Nations used to give each family a milk ration, and it provided an identity card that we had to present to be punched each day when we collected the milk. But not everyone wanted the milk, and those unclaimed rations turned into an opportunity for me. My mother gathered the cards of those who didn't want the milk and then would wake me at three in the morning so I could be first in line at the distribution center when it opened at six. I'd collect all the milk and then sell it for the highest price I could get to women who needed it to make yogurt, cheese, and other goods they could sell in Gaza City. The buyers were always in a hurry to get their milk, make their product, and get to the market in Gaza City, so a fast-moving, enthusiastic, and enterprising boy could make quite a bit of money in the early morning and still be on time for school.

Everything I earned was always for the good of my family. So if I managed to acquire something of my own, I guarded it as if it were gold. The school provided each student with a notebook, pencils, and an eraser, which felt like treasure—so much so that I kept all my belongings in a "school bag," which was actually an old flour bag with a string threaded through the top. The eraser was somehow very special, maybe because it was so small or maybe because my mother had never seen one before. In any case, to ensure that I wouldn't lose it, my mother put a hole in it and threaded it with a string so I could wear it around my neck. But I was a boy all the same: the eraser, precious as it was, became a toy I loved to take off my neck and swing through the air at the end of its string, higher and higher, watching it spin like a flying saucer. Then one day the string flew out of my fingers and disappeared into the crowd on the street. I was on my knees in a flash, searching everywhere, but I couldn't find it. I couldn't tell my mother that I'd lost the eraser. She would have thrashed me for sure. So I ran to the school, confessed to the teacher who had given it to me, and tearfully told him I was sorry. He gave me another one, just like the original, and sternly reminded me to be careful. He didn't have to worry, though; losing it once had been devastating enough.

In my neighborhood, we studied the Quran, learning it by heart so we could recite it in competitions. The first competition I won was during the festival of Ramadan when I was ten years old. The prize was presented by the Egyptian governor of the Gaza Strip, Ahmed Alajroudi. When my name was called to go up to the stage to receive the prize from this dignitary, I put my hand out and couldn't believe my good fortune when the governor handed me enough money to buy two weeks' worth of food for the family. Here was this truly poor child, wearing clothes that were patched together from rags, standing on the stage at the Jabalia Camp mosque receiving two and a half Egyptian pounds, about one U.S. dollar. That was a fortune in those days, considering that a state employee earned eight pounds a month. At about that time, my family was participating in a community fund. For a fee of fifty Egyptian piastres, or half an Egyptian pound, we'd get oil, butter, rice, and soup at cost. My earnings from the Quran competition would pay the fee for five weeks. I remember standing in line to fetch the goods for my mother, but when I got to the front and reached into my pocket to pay for the groceries, I discovered to my horror that I didn't have the money. Had it fallen through a hole in my pocket, which had been resewn so many times it wasn't reliable for holding the coins? Had someone stolen the money? All I knew was that it was gone and my mother was going to be very angry. I went home, dreading the thought of telling her what had happened.

I feared my mother as much as I loved her, and that day she beat me so much for losing the money I wondered if somehow she thought her blows would magically produce the money out of my flesh. Afterward she sent me back to the street to retrace my steps. I crawled about looking for the money under tables and behind stalls. I knew it wouldn't be there, but I was scared to go home again without it. As a boy, I could only wonder why she was doing this to me. Now I understand the level of frustration that wells up when you don't have enough to feed your kids, when life deals you one mean blow after another, when you feel that no matter how hard you work or how devoted you are, your efforts are fruitless. Desperation was the motivating force behind her anger, and sometimes the only targets she could find were the people she was trying to protect.

There were times when I hated my life, hated the misery we lived with, the filth and the poverty and being awakened at three o'clock in the morning out of a dead sleep to go to work. I hated myself for having to live like this, for not being able to change our circumstances no matter how hard I tried. In my culture the responsibility carried by the eldest son is very heavy. I was responsible for my parents as well as my younger brothers and sisters. I felt as though I was always living for someone else, never for myself. I railed against so many injustices when I was growing up, but today I look back and am thankful for getting through it at all, thankful for the teachers who saw a brighter future for me. I was lucky that so many of my teachers reached out to help me. They are the ones who boosted my energy and gave me the self-confidence to carry on. It was the teachers rather than my parents who opened doors for me and let me know there was a future apart from the grinding poverty in which we lived.

When people find out I grew up in an overcrowded refugee camp, they often ask me what it was like. They presume that even with all the deprivation and anxiety, young boys would still be young boys. How did we play? What sorts of fun did we have? Well, we locked friends in the outdoor toilet as a joke sometimes. We played other tricks and cavorted endlessly in the 104-degree heat with the water pipes on the street, spraying each other and unsuspecting passersby with blasts of water. Yet our games sometimes had perilous consequences. I was playing with the public water pipes that were outside our home. That's where we all got our water, and there were many spouts in a row. There was some glass on the ground at the base of one of the spouts. I was so caught up in playing with the water coming from the spout that one day I fell over it and sliced open my arm and my bare foot. My mother had to drop everything and take me to the United Nations health center to get the gash in my foot stitched, scolding me all the way.

The truth is, my most powerful memories of growing up in Jabalia Camp are of the stench of the latrine, the gnawing ache in my hungry stomach, the exhaustion from selling milk in the very early morning to earn that little bit of money that was so essential to my family, the anxiety I felt rushing to get to school on time. I had developed arthritic pain in my joints, and when I was tired, the pain in my legs was relentless. So even the fun was often not that much fun. It is true that the sky was always beautiful, but I don't remember marveling at sunsets or gazing at the dawn of a new day. Survival doesn't allow time for poetic reflection. In those years I was focused on one thing: getting an education and getting out of there.

Education was the only way out of the circumstances we were in. As the eldest son, I felt that I was the one to lead them, but it was hard. I would sit on the floor of our one-room house doing my homework by the light of an oil lamp as my younger siblings tussled about. I could tune out the noise and focus on the task, but sometimes concentration just wasn't enough. I recall one rainy evening when I was carefully printing the answers to my homework, as I always kept in mind how important tidiness was to my teachers, and suddenly there was a drop of water on the paper, then another, and soon the words were blurring and blotching and running down the page. Raindrops leaking through the roof had spoiled my homework, and I had to start again.

There was no summer camp or team sports or videos in my formative years. Mostly they weren't available, but I was also exclusively focused on learning, and when I wasn't in class or studying, I was earning money in order to stay in school.

My mother was like a lioness when it came to protecting us, but she never relented on how much she demanded of us. She expected me to give as much as she did to the effort of improving our situation, and when I failed, I paid for it with beatings. The Palestinian mother is the author of the survival story of the Palestinian people. She is the heroine, the one behind the successes. She feeds everyone before taking food for herself. She never gives up, and she pushes against the barriers holding her children back. For my mother, survival was always paramount. School was important, but it didn't carry the same value as a job. If I could earn money, she would encourage me to skip classes to do it.

There was one curious incident that stays in my memory, although I didn't fully comprehend what had happened to me until I was an adult. In 1966, a year before the Six Day War would end the Egyptian administration of Gaza and replace it with the Israeli occupation, my cousin on my mother's side invited me to go to Egypt with him. (The Six Day War of June 5–10, 1967, was a war between Israel and the neighboring states of Egypt, Jordan, and Syria. The Arab states of Iraq, Saudi Arabia, Sudan, Tunisia, Morocco, and Algeria also contributed troops and arms. At the war's end, Israel had gained control of the Sinai Peninsula, the Gaza Strip, the West Bank, East Jerusalem, and the Golan Heights.) I was eleven years old and absolutely ecstatic about the idea of going to Egypt. My cousin was a trader, my mother told me, and he took goods from Gaza to sell across the border in Egypt. I had enormous dreams for what I would see on this trip to Cairo: the pyramids, the anniversary celebrations of President Gamal Abdel Nasser that everyone was talking about, and I desperately wanted to go to the zoo. I had never been outside Jabalia Camp except to go for a day to Gaza City. I had only seen photos of zoo animals and the pyramids in picture books. President Nasser was discussed all the time; Nasser this and Nasser that. Imagine, I could see this man that everyone talked about.

My cousin prepared me carefully for the trip across the border. My mother gave me a special jacket to wear, into which she'd sewn extra pockets. She also gave me a pair of size nine shoes that were much too large for me. My cousin stuffed the pockets inside the jacket and the oversized shoes with many pairs of socks he wanted to trade. I didn't have a clue what he was up to and thought it was just a clever way for one person to carry a lot of items. What I didn't realize was that Gaza was a duty-free zone and my cousin was trying to avoid paying taxes when he crossed into Egypt in order to keep the cost of his goods low. I also thought I was helping him with his job, which in fact I was, and felt very grown-up to be selected for the task.

My cousin set off to Egypt with one of his partners by car, and he put me on the train that would go across the border accompanied by his other partner. When the customs officer came onto the train to inspect the passengers and their parcels and asked me if I was bringing in anything that needed to be declared, I confidently said, "No." The truth is, I didn't know what he was talking about. The officer didn't believe me, opened up my jacket, and found all the socks. He smacked me across the side of the head. I didn't know what I'd done wrong, and now he was holding me by the ear and yelling at me. I was scared to death. There was another man sitting in the same train compartment, a military man, a peacekeeper from India, who took pity on me and said, "Let the kid go." When my cousin's partner augmented that request with a small amount of cash, the officer did. I shook for the rest of the journey to Cairo.

When I got off the train in the city, I could hardly believe what my eyes were feasting upon. There was no electricity in Jabalia Camp, but the city of Cairo was a festival of lights. I thought I had arrived in the capital of the world, or gone from under the ground all the way up to the moon. It was colorful, noisy, and, in the eyes of a child, a glorious sight. But, as I soon found out, I would have no time to enjoy this grand city. My cousin's partner took me to a low-rent hotel, where we rejoined my cousin. This was where the traders did business with the locals, and that's where I stayed the whole time, watching the customers come and go, sitting around while my cousin carried out his business. So on my one trip out of Gaza as a child, I smuggled goods for my cousin. What's more, he knowingly sent me into danger, from which I was saved only by the efforts of an Indian military man and the bribe from my cousin's partner. My only reward? I got a watermelon from Ismailia, capital of Egypt's Canal region and renowed for its melons, which I brought back to my family. When I told my mother what happened, she laughed as if she'd known all along that I was being used as a courier.

When I got back from that misadventure, I continued with my survival routine—going to school and trying to earn a few piastres for the family. I sold ice cream and seeds and geraniums after school. I accepted any work that came along, and never tasted the sweetness of a summer holiday. For a while I had a job at a brick factory, where I had to line up bricks, water them down so they'd harden, and carry them to a pallet and stack them. I was paid two piastres for every hundred bricks I stacked. I worked there after school every afternoon until the factory closed. Consider that there are one hundred piastres in an Egyptian pound and it takes about two and a half Egyptian pounds to make a U.S. dollar. Hauling those bricks didn't give me much, but I took what I could get, and though sometimes I was reluctant (what child wouldn't want to keep some of the money he earned), I always handed the money over to my mother.

School was the place where I got my rewards. In 1967, when I was in the sixth grade, I was selected to become the school broadcaster, which was tantamount to being elected class president. The teacher prepared the news each day, and I read it over the intercom for the entire term. I liked that. I liked almost everything about school, because the teachers—not all of them, but the most important ones—convinced me that with an education I could do anything I wanted. I worked very hard to earn their praise, to stay at the top of the class. I remember the June day when the results for the final exams for all grade six students in Gaza were supposed to be announced; it was the day the Six Day War started. At first I was more upset about not hearing the results of my exams than about having to endure a war. Perhaps it was because I understood so little of actual war when it started. But I learned. It wasn't the first war of my lifetime, but I was only an infant during the Suez Crisis, also referred to as the Tripartite Aggression or Sinai War, in which Britain, France, and Israel attacked Egypt on October 26, 1956. Egypt and Israel had been sparring with each other since 1948, when Israel declared nationhood. My father told me the entire region was on tenterhooks the whole time, that there was always a border dispute or the threat of attack. So people weren't surprised when the Sinai conflict actually began, sparked by Egypt's decision to nationalize the Suez Canal after the withdrawal of an offer by Britain and the United States to fund the construction of the Aswan Dam. People just didn't know what shape the war would take, how it would alter their lives. But like most wars, not much was accomplished in the Sinai War of 1956 that would change the way of life in Gaza, except that it was a brutal episode that led to six months of occupation by Israel. In the aftermath, Gaza formally came under Egyptian administration, a state of affairs that would last eleven years. (Later I would learn that it was during this war that the Egyptian leader Gamal Abdel Nasser rose to prominence and that this was also when the United States established itself as the chief negotiator in the Middle East.)

The Six Day War of 1967 was something very different. From my twelve-year-old perspective, it came out of nowhere. I was waiting impatiently for the grade six exam results to be posted at the school, as I wanted to see my name at the head of the class. But instead, my Palestinian teachers were so preoccupied by the growing tension between Egypt and Israel that they only posted a pass-or-fail list. Although there was always plenty of talk among the adults about avenging the 1948 Nakba, to me, a schoolboy who was forever on the hunt for a job that would pay cash or in-kind donations to feed my family, such talk was merely background noise. Then the whispering about war in the refugee camp turned into loud cheering that this war was going to be a total defeat of the Israelis. It wasn't.

It started on June 5 and ended on June 10. In a mere six days, the Israelis destroyed the Egyptian air force before the planes even got off the ground, and turned back the neighboring armies of Egypt, Jordan, and Syria, and the Arab states of Iraq, Saudi Arabia, Sudan, Tunisia, Morocco, and Algeria, all of which had contributed arms or soldiers to the battle.

It was actually unfinished business that led to the war. After the 1956 Sinai War, peacekeepers had been left behind to keep the warring factions apart. In May 1967, Gamal Abdel Nasser requested the withdrawal of the United Nations peacekeepers from Egyptian territory and the Gaza Strip. He closed the Straits of Tiran to any ship flying the Israeli flag or carrying materials that could be used for war. Arab countries fell in line to support the Egyptian initiative. Israel called up seventy thousand reservists, and its cabinet voted to launch an offensive, which led to a standoff of several weeks. Then full-out war began, and in an astonishingly small number of days, Israel had won—and had assumed control of the Sinai Peninsula, the Gaza Strip, the West Bank, East Jerusalem, and the Golan Heights.

Although I was not aware of it at the time, this disruption in my community was pivotal in various capitals around the world, the evidence being the number of names by which the Six Day War is still known. The Arabic name is Harb 1967. (*Harb* means "war" in Arabic.) Six Day War in Hebrew is Milhemet Sheshet Ha-Yamim. The rest of the world, divided into supporters of one side or the other, calls it a variety of names: the 1967 Arab-Israeli War, the Third Arab-Israeli War, or a Naksah. (*Naksah* means "setback.")

The Six Day War affects the geopolitics of the region to this day, but it wasn't those geopolitical consequences that made the war a milestone in my life. I was only twelve years old. The war was not something that happened on a transistor radio or was described by way of the rumor mill at the refugee camp. It happened right in front of my eyes, and it looked like the end of the world to me.

Israeli tanks rolled right onto our street. The shelling, the shooting, and the fires breaking out all over the camp were utterly terrifying. Parents were fleeing, some leaving their children behind. There was chaos, noise, and panic. Most of my family headed for a fruit farm in Beit Lahia, north of Jabalia Camp. Hundreds of others did the same, but when we got there, we realized that some of the children had become separated from their families and some family members hadn't come at all. The effort to escape was so disjointed that some of my own brothers had been left behind. Parents, including my own, started screaming. There was absolute pandemonium.

We stayed in the fields for three or four days, slept on the ground, and ate the apples and apricots in the orchards until it was over. When we returned cautiously to our homes, we found out that some people who'd had no place to run had dug holes in the ground, jumped in, and covered themselves with pieces of tin. Many of our neighbors were killed or missing. We also discovered that the Israel Defense Forces were now occupying Gaza. There were tanks all over the streets and soliders who pointed their guns at us while we walked home. I had never seen Israeli soldiers before. When loudspeakers suddenly announced that all the residents should gather at the public square in the middle of Jabalia Camp, I was certain we were all going to be killed. The square was also the major water collection basin for rainwater and sewage for the whole camp, but since this was summertime, the water hole was dry. The soldiers made us line up around the empty water hole. I was sure we would be forced to jump into it and be shot. But all the soldiers did was arrest some young men I didn't know and take them away to prison. Then they told us to return to our houses and not to break any of the rules, the major one being that from now on, there would be a curfew from six P.M. until six A.M. For me, that was the end of the Six Day War.

Almost no one had behaved the way I had expected them to behave; not the parents who had run off without their children, not the soldiers who I had presumed were there to kill us. The knowledge unsettled me. It made me more aware of what people say versus what they actually do. I finally realized that my own poverty wasn't the only reality holding me back. I began to ask questions about discrimination: Why are the Israelis like this and we are like that? How come there's a difference in the way we are treated? At last, at age twelve, I began to keep my eyes open in order to better understand the circumstances under which I was living.

Soon enough, after the Six Day War, Israelis started visiting parts of the Gaza Strip that had always flourished; the areas where Gazans had lived before the refugees arrived. The fish and the fresh fruits and vegetables in the region were particularly attractive for these Israeli tourists. I saw their arrival as a way to earn some money. I carried their shopping bags and fetched parcels of fruit for them. I'd walk the almost four miles from Jabalia Camp to Gaza City with a basket strapped to my shoulders and earn a little money that way.

When the new school year started in September 1967, for the first time I began to have doubts about my goals. Why was I bothering with school when we were occupied and the future seemed so bleak? I was older now and better understood the consequences of occupation. My school grades notwithstanding, I began to question whether there really was a way out of this turmoil. Also, my family desperately needed any money I could earn, and I was good at finding jobs. Why shouldn't I just try to make life a little easier for my family? As the eldest boy, it was my job to provide. Perhaps I should give up on my dream of improving our lives through education.

So, in grade seven, I started skipping classes. If there was a job to do, I wouldn't go to school. If I was exhausted from piling orange crates until three in the morning, I would rest rather than attend classes. My parents knew I was missing school, but they both thought that it was better to work and make money than to get an education. I had always tried to set an example for my brothers and sisters, but for a time I didn't care about that at all.

Then my English teacher took me aside. He told me I was a good student, said I was intelligent enough that I could eventually go to a university and become a professional: a doctor, a lawyer, or an engineer. He pleaded with me to consider the consequences of skipping school. At that point I had actually been planning to drop out, but after he took me to task, I decided that I couldn't let him down, though I continued to skip class when it was absolutely necessary. My family obliga-tions pressed on me like a red-hot branding iron, but my teachers never stopped encouraging me to stay the course. I tried my best to keep my teachers happy, especially my English teacher. It was the practice to assign extra homework for students to do over the regular two-week winter break, which for me was an opportunity to work at a paying job every day that I couldn't miss. So in grade eight, when the winter holiday rolled around, I did all my English homework in advance and handed it in to be marked before the holiday had even started. I will thank my teachers forever for being relentless in their encouragement to stay in school.

By the end of grade eight, I rarely skipped classes, but I never stopped working either. In the winter months there were always jobs picking citrus fruits and loading them onto trucks. In the summer months I would go to the farms to load fertilizer. This entailed piling manure into two baskets that were slung over my shoulders and carrying the load to a truck. I felt like a donkey. The smell was awful, the summer heat almost unbearable, and the manure seemed to weigh more than I did.

I remember I had to walk the three- or four-mile distance to the farm. This meant I had to get up very early to make it there by six, when work started. All that walking back and forth was hard on my arthritic legs, and my joints became swollen and inflamed. One day I fell and couldn't get up. My legs just could not support me. The United Nations health center referred me to Al-Shifa hospital in Gaza City.

I asked the doctors and nurses so many questions about the arthritic pain in my legs. That's where I learned about the use of high-dose aspirin for my condition and about everything else I could think of. All of it fascinated me. They were all Palestinians like me; I wanted to know what they knew, live like they seemed to live, with good jobs and the respect of those around them. I knew one of the doctors had running water in his house and a special room called a sitting room where people gathered just to visit. But more than that, I was very impressed by the medical treatments, by the fact that there were drugs or therapies or other means to actually alter the course of an illness. I could see that they were really helping people. This was when and where my dream about becoming a doctor began. I could see that if I became a doctor, it would be possible for me to improve the condition of my family and also to serve the Palestinian people.

However, the hospital experience left other impressions on me as well. I shared a room with a Palestinian girl whose family brought her food—quantities of food such as I'd never seen in my life. They obviously weren't refugees! They brought whole bunches of bananas. If there was ever a banana in our house, my mother would cut it into equal pieces—one for each child. In my world there was no such thing as a bunch of bananas, and certainly nothing as luxurious as a whole banana for yourself. The girl and I shared a cupboard in the hospital room, and one night I took one of her bananas and ate it. I loved that banana. I admit I stole the fruit, but I excused the act by telling myself that the Quran allows such behavior if you are hungry.

Another lasting impression was made by the relationships I observed between the male and female nurses and the doctors. It was clear even to this young boy that they were having fun at work. They respected each other, worked hard, and helped each other out. The hospital culture—the way the women and men related to each other—was very different from what I experienced at home. For example, there was teasing and gossip about nurses and doctors having intimate relations. In my world, men and women wouldn't even work together, never mind make jokes like this with each other. I saw romantic relationships between men and women in the health field, and they looked normal to me. Where I came from, in the refugee camp, on my street, in my village, this would not be seen as normal at all.

When I was fifteen years old, I had the chance to work in Israel for the summer, on a farm called Moshav Hodaia, close to the town of Ashqelon. It was owned by the Madmoony family. For forty days I lived in the heart of a Jewish family farm. I did chores from six in the morning until eight at night, working pretty much every daylight hour. I had never slept away from home before, except on that trip to Cairo, and I was so lonely that I can remember the aching in my gut to this day. Yet the family, Sephardic Jews, were very warm to me, even when I did really naïve things that they must have found perplexing. For instance, I was still dressing in hand-me-down clothes, donations from the humanitarian agencies that operated in Gaza. I had assumed that the clothes came to us because their former owners were so rich they threw their clothes away when they got tired of wearing them. So when I saw some piles of clothing on the floor of the Madmoony household, I assumed they were throwing the clothes away, and I quickly gathered them and stored them in my knapsack so I could take them home to my mother. I had no idea I was actually collecting the family laundry! After a while they asked me if I'd seen their clothing, and to my great embarrassment I had to confess.

That summer left a powerful impression on me in many ways. That an Israeli family would hire me, treat me fairly, and show so much kindness toward me was completely unexpected. The experience was made all the more unforgettable by the events that followed one week after my return to Gaza.

We were dirt-poor refugees who had by this time moved out of the one-room shelter in which we'd been crammed and into a simple two-bedroom house in Block P-42 of Jabalia Camp, with a roof made from small cement tiles that would still leak whenever it rained. The public toilets, shared by several families, were still outside. Even though it was barely fit for human habitation, it was our home.

At the time, Ariel Sharon was the Israeli military commander of the Gaza Strip. He was concerned that the roads that ran through the camp weren't wide enough for his tanks to patrol. His solution? Bulldoze hundreds of houses to the ground. There wasn't a thing we could do. The level of inhumanity was astonishing, and it has stayed with me to this day. That it was Ariel Sharon who ordered this destruction meant even more to our family as our land in Houg had been taken by him. So when his tanks came to our street that night, my family shuddered at the thought of what could happen to us. The warning sound of their tracks crunching up the road awakened everyone. It was midnight. Families rushed to doorways to see long guns pointing at us from the turrets of the tanks. Now I wonder how those soldiers must have felt, pointing their murderous weapons at little children still rubbing sleep from their eyes and clinging to their mothers in doorways. Even then, I recognized it as the quintessential display of power over the powerless. The houses along the street were simple, small, even primitive, but they were all we had. Sharon saw them simply as obstructions on a road that he wanted widened. I remember the feeling of being trapped, of peril coming to my home. Whatever type of house you have, if you have a house, it means you are not homeless. Thirty-eight years later, when I witnessed the destruction of Gaza during the Israeli incursion of December 2008 and January 2009, the same thought occurred to me. I saw people become homeless as bombs smashed into their dwellings and brought them tumbling down, and I realized that the pain of homelessness has never left me.

The soliders ordered the people on my street to leave our houses and stand together and wait. About eight hours went by. At dawn they said we had a couple of hours to empty our houses. I was thinking, "Empty? There's nothing inside to empty." Whatever difficulties we had with this house, there was nothing to save except the house itself, its walls. A lush, tangled grapevine had bloomed and grown for years over the door. We appreciated it most in the summer months when the temperature soared to 104 degrees Fahrenheit and the inside of the house was unbearably hot. The whole family would sleep outside under that grapevine. So when the soldiers said, "Empty the house," I wondered how one could pluck up a grapevine and move it to another location.

They wanted us to move to Al 'Arīsh, a town in the northern part of the Sinai Desert, where there were empty houses because the Egyptians who had lived there had run away when the Israelis arrived and occupied the region. But how were we to do that? We were Palestinians. We grew up in the Jabalia refugee camp. This small house was our home, our palace. Couldn't anyone understand how important it was to us? It protected us from the winter cold, the rain; it gave us a place to be together, to rest, to eat.

We decided to stay. But because we refused to relocate, Sharon denied us compensation for our home. The blackmail was astounding. He would have paid us for our house if we'd agreed to be uprooted illegally and moved to a place we didn't know, where we didn't have family. About five families from our street agreed to move, but they returned a few months later. That day I learned the bitter lesson of what it means to be helpless in the face of one man's power.

The bulldozers started their calamitous work on our street at eight A.M.. We scrambled to collect falling bricks, to try to salvage something in order to build another place. In one hour we witnessed the demolition of our house and about a hundred others that were in the way of the tanks. Many more houses throughout the refugee camp were also demolished under orders from Sharon in a campaign that lasted for two weeks. Then the soliders rumbled back down the road in their malignant columns of tanks that had knocked down our lives. Was our suffering of any consequence to their consciences? Did they see us as victims? Or were we simply nameless, faceless humans who were in their way?

That night and for several nights thereafter, we slept in one room at my uncle's house. My parents and siblings slept in a row on the floor, like pickets on a fence. I was stretched out at everyone else's feet. Our few possessions were stacked in a box outside the door as there was no space in the room to keep them with us. I wasn't a little kid anymore; I had worked outside the country earning my own money. Sleeping at everyone's feet felt humiliating, and I smarted from both the cause and the effect. But I did have a plan. I'd earned 400 lira (the Israeli currency at the time; about US$140) working on the Madmoony farm that summer. Along with a few Egyptian pounds my mother had saved, we had enough to buy another house. My father had been ill while I was away in Israel; now it broke my heart to see him witness the destruction of the only shelter his family had.

But I knew he was pleased and proud that his son had come home with enough money to solve this enormous problem. My brothers were also very impressed with me, and to this day they tell people how I bought the family a house when I was just fifteen years old.

The new house was not much better than our old one. Yet it was from inside this home, built on destruction, that I was able to reflect on the second milestone in my life. The paradox between the warm hospitality of the Israeli family who had employed me that summer and the brute force of Sharon's Israeli soldiers made me recognize that I had to commit myself to finding a peaceful bridge between the divides.

I had seen the destruction of my home, and to this day those images stay with me, but hate has never been part of my repertoire, nor were politics at that time. Of course I knew about Fatah and the Palestine Liberation Organization, and I was never accused of not being engaged. The PLO developed a charter in 1968 containing the resolutions of the Palestine National Council. The text of the charter contains thirty-three articles, the first of which states that Palestine is the homeland of the Arab Palestinian people; it is an indivisible part of the Arab homeland, and the Palestinian people are an integral part of the Arab nation. Part of the charter speaks of the Palestinian identity, saying that the Palestinian identity is a genuine, essential, and inherent characteristic; it is transmitted from parents to children.

Of course, it was important to me to support what the council was saying, so during the school year I went with my brothers and friends to the demonstrations in support of the PLO, but I always returned to class afterward. I was very aware of the suffering of my people, but I also believed the weapon I needed was not a rock or a gun but an education so that I could fight for human rights and help all the Palestinian people. Even though I sometimes attended marches organized by Fatah and the PLO, political demonstrations were not a large part of my day-to-day life as a teenager. Except for my brother Noor, my siblings were not very interested either. Resistance to occupation was discussed in our home, but my parents were not involved in politics. Politics were not considered a big deal.

I would hear the news on the streets, and though I was never involved, I was also never accused of not being engaged. To clearly understand the circumstances of life in Gaza requires an understanding of Fatah and the PLO. When the state of Israel was founded in 1948, the Palestinian people were also without a homeland. Although there had been talk for decades that Palestinians would have to make way for an Israeli state, I think most Palestinians were in denial that such a thing would ever really happen. The first Palestinian National Council, which included representatives from Palestinian communities in Jordan, the West Bank, the Gaza Strip, Syria, Lebanon, Kuwait, Iraq, Egypt, Qatar, Libya, and Algeria, met in Jerusalem on May 29, 1964, and established the Palestine Liberation Organization at the conclusion of the meeting on June 2, 1964. Its mission was the liberation of Palestine through armed struggle. The original PLO charter called for the creation of a Palestine with boundaries that had existed at the time of the British mandate, claiming that this was an integral regional unit. In addition, the PLO called for the return of refugees displaced by Israel and, most important, for self-determination for Palestinians. Egypt's President Nasser had argued for a long time that Arabs should live in one state, but not all Arab leaders agreed. At the meetings

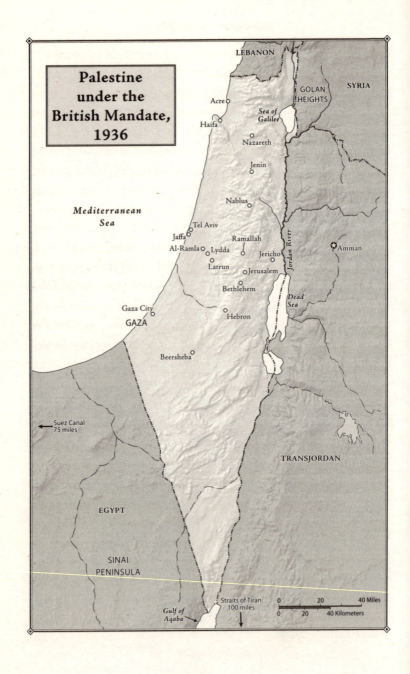

Palestine
under the
British Mandate,
1936

LEBANON

SYRIA

GOLAN
HEIGHTS

Acre

Sea of
Galilee

Haifa

Nazareth

Jenin

Mediterranean
Sea

Nablus

Tel Aviv

Jaffa

Ramallah

Al-Ramla

Lydda

Jericho

Latrun

Jerusalem

Jordan River

Amman

Bethlehem

Dead
Sea

Gaza City

GAZA

Hebron

Beersheba

Suez Canal
75 miles

TRANSJORDAN

EGYPT

SINAI
PENINSULA

Straits of Tiran
100 miles

0   20   40 Miles

Gulf of
Aqaba

0   20   40 Kilometers

held during the midsixties, the suggestions for borders of the proposed Palestinian state were like an early warning signal of the trouble that would come. For example, rather than being an autonomous state, the West Bank would be controlled by the Hashemite Kingdom of Jordan, and the Gaza Strip would similarly not have any internal government that interfered with the Egyptian administration. In short, the Arab countries surrounding Palestine would enrich their own geography, and the Palestinians would be ruled by Jordanians and Egyptians rather than by the Israelis.

Of course, from school, from conversations on the street and at home, I knew the leaders' names. Ahmad Shukeiri led the PLO from June 1964 to the December after the Six Day War in 1967. He was followed by Yahya Hammuda (December 24, 1967 to February 2, 1969), then by Yasser Arafat, who held on to power until he died on November 11, 2004, when Mahmoud Abbas took over.

As for Fatah, it had been founded by members of the Palestinian diaspora in 1954. The name Fatah is an acronym comprising the first letter of each of the words of the full name of the movement: حركة التحرير الوطني الفلسطيني) arakat al-ta rīr al-wa anī al-filas īnī), which means "Liberation Organization of the Palestinian Nation." In Arabic the acronym means "opening" or "conquering" or "victory," and it reflects the organization's ideology of liberating Palestine. Yasser Arafat, who was chairman of the General Union of Palestinian Students at that time, was one of the founders of Fatah, and his position in these two organizations made it possible for him to subsequently ascend to the chairmanship of the PLO.

After the Six Day War, Fatah became the dominant force in Palestinian politics. It joined forces with the PLO in 1967, and to this day Fatah is the largest member of the PLO and carries the most influence on the council. I was aware of all this as a teenager, but I wasn't preoccupied with it. We had no radio and no TV. I heard talk on the street about the new leaders, but to be honest, it was wise to be careful about what you said and did. For example, it was illegal to fly a Palestinian flag, and you could be arrested for supporting the PLO or if you were caught listening to the hour-long broadcast in which Fatah Radio transmitted its message every evening.

There has always been a pecking order in Gaza. Some Palestinians lived in the region before refugees started arriving in 1948. And although the refugees soon outnumbered the local population, the latter had roots there and we didn't. We didn't depend on them for jobs, and at first they didn't see us as Gazans. From 1948 to 1967, the Gaza Strip was under Egyptian administration. The United Nations, after it arrived in 1949, provided primary health care, elementary school education, and social support (rations of food, cooking oil, donated clothes). The rest—high school, tertiary health care, police, security, passport control, and general administration—was all run by the Egyptians. After the Six Day War, the Israelis replaced the Egyptians as the de facto government. Although the high school I went to was run at first by the Egyptians and then by the Israeli military, the teachers were always Palestinian. Alliances were constantly being made and remade between various groups. It wasn't something that interested me, but everyone learned at an early age that there were people to respect and pay attention to and others who had no connections.

In 1970, when I was fifteen years old, I started my secondary school education at El Faloja high school. I became a serious student again as well as a voracious reader. If there were books around, I grabbed them. I preferred novels to politics, but not just for entertainment; I wanted to strengthen my grasp of the Arabic language. Reading became my passion.

I kept working diligently at whatever jobs I could find. Now, because I was older, these jobs tended to be better. For instance, I sorted oranges by size at the same place where I used to wash them, pack them in crates, and stack the crates for transportation. Sorting by size paid more and also put me in a position to get extra pay on the side. The orange crates would fall apart and need repair, so whenever the sorting was slow, I'd pick up some more money repairing the crates. After the Israelis imposed their curfew, I couldn't leave the factory in time to get home, so I'd sleep there with the other boys. In the morning we'd wash our faces with water out of a bucket at the back of the factory and head to school, which provided a rudimentary breakfast, milk, and vitamins to the students. I remember being very hungry and always tired.

One morning when the teacher had lined us up in class, I felt dizzy and faint. I tried to stay on my feet, but everything started to spin and I collapsed to the floor. The teacher came to my aid. My teachers knew about the long hours I worked. They knew there wasn't enough food at home. I don't know how I would have managed without them.

Of all the awful jobs I undertook, there was only one that I really hated. When I was old enough, I was able to get construction work in the city of Ashqelon in Israel, which was very close to Gaza. I loathed that work: the hot sun blistering my back, the heavy lifting, the relentless pace. But I took it because I could make good money—the best money I ever made as a teenager. An apartment building was being constructed in the southern part of Ashqelon; I was part of the crew on Fridays and holidays for the entire year I was sixteen years old.

I imagine it would be hard for anyone who hasn't lived in Gaza to understand our lives. We were everything the word *refugee* stands for: disenfranchised, dismissed, marginalized, and suffering.

My mother wanted so badly for us to succeed. I would sometimes challenge her because it all seemed so hopeless. How was I supposed to succeed when I had to work all afternoon into the evening and again every morning; when I had no materials for studying, and when I had to do my homework by the light of a kerosene lamp while sitting on the concrete floor, hoping it wouldn't rain because the leaking roof would splatter my papers and I'd have to start all over again? She always turned a deaf ear to my complaints and would admonish me if ever I wasn't first in the class. She was equally tough on the other kids in the family, but the majority of parents were like that; the hardness of life affected the way they behaved with their children. I remember crying once when someone else had higher marks than me in math. I wonder today what those tears were about. Did they come from fear—that if I wasn't first, I might never get out of this grinding poverty? Were my tears really my ego? Was excelling academically the only source of pride I had, the only dignity I could muster? I look back at that time and wonder. But when I look back, I also see the woman who demanded that I succeed no matter what obstacles I faced, and I hear the teacher who told me to dry my tears: Ahmed Al Halaby, my first-grade teacher who made me feel anything was possible. I learned from both of them that I was on the right path, and I cherish and honor their memories.

Of the nine children in our family, the family of the second wife, there are eight high school graduates, of whom four are also university graduates, including a pharmacist, a public relations professional, a teacher, and me, a doctor. We owe my mother credit for our successes, even though she was forced by circumstances to view survival as ultimately more important than education. I think unemployment and poverty contributed to what I would call an unhealthy manner of parenting. Yet because she saw to it that we survived, we succeeded.

I graduated from high school in 1974. I had applied for a scholarship and eventually was admitted to the University of Cairo to continue my studies. I realize that it wasn't until I was leaving home to go to Cairo that the family of the first wife and the family of the second wife actually came together in any meaningful way. I was the first person among the Abuelaishes to be accepted at a university. My departure for Cairo was a major event for my brothers and sisters, the whole family, and indeed everyone from my family's home village of Houg. There had been only four students from Jabalia Camp accepted to study medicine.

Everyone in my family came to say good-bye, even my half-brothers. One of them traveled all the way from Saudi Arabia to be there that day. They came to ask if I needed anything, to say they were proud of me, and to wish me good luck. This personal coming together helped me realize that sometimes it's better to look forward, to move into the future, rather than dwell on the past. And there was so much to look forward to. But I carried the questions that had dogged me since childhood into the wider world. How come a Palestinian child does not live like an Israeli child? Why do Palestinian children have to toil at any hard job just to be able to go to school? How is it that when we are sick, we can't get the medical help Israeli kids take for granted? I continued to wonder about the divide between Israelis and Palestinians, and why it seemed as if it couldn't be repaired. We were people more like each other than not, and though I was young and ignorant, my experiences at jobs in Israel had instilled in me a sense of pride that had become something of a mantra: "I am a Palestinian from the Jabalia refugee camp in the Gaza Strip, and I am the same as you."

THREE

Finding My Way

In 1975, I left Gaza to accept my scholarship at the University of Cairo and began the long journey toward a medical degree. This adventure would move me one step closer to my dream of escaping the poverty that was choking my family. I was excited and full of anticipation about this next stage in my life. The scholarship was a doorway to the world, a ticket to learning, which had become my passion. I felt like I was at the beginning of a journey I had been praying for since I was a young child.

I had applied for the scholarship during my last year of high school. The University of Cairo accepted two hundred Palestinian students every year in twenty different faculties, including medicine, engineering, pharmacy, teaching, and law. I had top grades, so I hoped I could get into the school of medicine, but I applied to every faculty just in case. The way the system worked was that you applied and then waited a full year after high school before you learned whether or not you had been accepted. I would need money for room and board in Cairo, so for that year I worked every day I could in Israel.

The border between Gaza and Israel was open at that time, so it was easy to cross back and forth on a daily basis; you only had to present your identification card at a gateway, and the Israeli official would wave you through. That meant I could save money by living at home, but it also meant I had to leave early every morning to be in Ashqelon in time to line up with other laborers at a downtown square where employers picked workers for the day. I was young enough and cocky enough to promote myself to the prospective employers at this hawkers' market, telling them I was strong, knowledgeable, and hard-working. I did every sort of job they offered—factory jobs, or work in agriculture or construction, both of which I hated because they meant sweating in the sun. Some days, no matter how hard I tried to sell my services, there was no work, and I'd have to go home empty-handed. No work meant no help for the family, no savings for the university, and I took these rejections to heart.

I also learned that at times something good can come out of something bad. For example, one day a man was looking for two workers to build a chicken coop. It was a two-day job. He picked me and another guy, but the second morning I was late getting to the square, I can't remember why. I do remember running breathless to the pickup point and seeing the other worker go off with his cousin to do the job I'd been hired for. I shouted at him and started berating him for giving my job to his cousin. I felt stung by the injustice, the loss of a work-day, but another Israeli employer who had been watching the drama said, "Forget it, come and work for me. I am also building a chicken coop, but it's more than a two-day job." I ended up working for that man for almost eight months. He had a contract to build chicken coops for his customers all over the district. He not only showed me how to wire the chicken coop but also taught me how to install the electricity and the water system, to stain the metal exterior with rust repellent. It was a bonanza of learning for me. After two or three months he made me the manager. I brought boys from my neighborhood to work with us and paid them as well as myself on contract rather than taking a salary. That way you get more work done, and everyone works even harder because they can see the money to be made. I worked for him right up to the day I left for Cairo. He even gave me a good-bye present.

I remember the moment I left Gaza for Cairo as if it was yesterday. I had been accepted into the medical school, and it was an emotional and triumphant day for all of us. My mother wanted to be the mother of a doctor as much as I wanted to follow my dream of joining the field of medicine. I felt drawn to the profession as profoundly as a person is attached to his name. My heart was pounding. My clothes were packed in a blue plastic suitcase. I carried a satchel stuffed with olives, soap, red chili peppers, and my mother's homemade bread and cakes. I waved to my family, who were weeping with joy, from the steps of the Israeli bus that would take me and the other students through the Sinai into Egypt.

The windows of the bus were painted over so that we couldn't see outside, because we were traveling though the Israeli-occupied Sinai and the Israelis didn't want us to see their military installations. Once at the Egyptian border, the Red Cross organized the transfer to an Egyptian bus, which took us to a quarantine camp where our vaccination certificates were checked and each of us was examined in case we were bringing a communicable disease into Egypt, a procedure that took several days. At last we moved to the student quarters in Cairo.

Arriving in Cairo as a student was unbelievably exciting. I wanted to see and do everything at once. In Gaza, there were no shops or cafés like this, no music blaring from loudspeakers. However, I no sooner arrived than I had to leave. The particular campus I was assigned to was sixty-two miles away. I was terribly disappointed until I found out that, if my marks were good enough, I could transfer at the end of the first year to the Cairo campus. I took an apartment with two other students and started classes, determined to get top marks.

There was a Palestinian girl in my class who flirted with me. She was very beautiful, and I always saved a seat for her next to me. I liked her, but her behavior also distressed me. I wondered what she wanted. Was I to have a romance in Egypt? The thought shocked me; so much so, that I decided I wouldn't go out to the parties, not even to the cinema; I would study day and night to reach my goal. The girl approached me a few more times and I was cordial with her, but I was scared of a relationship that might become more than friendship. I was young.

I made the grade academically, and the next year I moved to the Cairo campus and began to taste life in a big international city. I wanted to memorize every corner of this place. I did break down and go to clubs with my friends, although I never drank alcohol, and still don't. I connected with students from half a dozen other Arab countries, joined the foreign students' club, talked about politics and girls into the middle of the night, and had my eyes opened to the world beyond the small refugee camp where I was raised. I didn't have a girlfriend, but my colleagues tease me to this day about the life we lived as students—carousing from party to party and staying out until dawn.

While the parties were a lot of fun, I never lost sight of my priority—my coursework. While we were required to study and to practice in each of the various medical rotations such as pediatrics, internal medicine, and surgery, it was obstetrics and gynecology and their relation to the miracle of life that energized me as though, when I was studying this subject, I was breathing rarefied air. The first time I assisted in the delivery of a newborn, I was mesmerized. That a life had just begun at my fingertips, that the woman on the delivery table had come through this nine-month period safely and was grinning with love, joy, and pride, was a miracle to me. From that day on, I saw pregnancy as a process as natural as eating and drinking. Later, during my internship in Cairo, I knew I wanted to specialize in this field. Delivering a baby thrilled me. A mother would be screaming during the delivery and swearing she would never do this again, and then she'd say afterward, "I bet I'll see you in another year or two." I remember the first time I treated a woman who was hemorrhaging during a miscarriage. She could have died. I managed to get the bleeding under control and saved her life. Using my skills to save a life or help a patient in distress or bring a newborn into the world was what I became most excited about.

Another key part of my Cairo experience that stays with me was our student celebrations of Ramadan. About fifteen of us would gather and share food at each other's houses. Then we would go out into the Cairo night and join the festivities: the singing and storytelling in places like the Al-Azhar club until the sun came up. Those were carefree, precious days unlike anything I had known before, or have enjoyed since.

After one preparatory year, another five years of medical school, and a year interning at Cairo University Hospital, I graduated with my M.D. in 1983, seven years after the adventure began, and received my license to be a general practitioner. I was young, passionate, and ready to work. But after what I'd been through as a kid growing up in Gaza, I also saw myself as a conduit that could bring news of life in the refugee camp to the outside world. Someone had to start paying attention to what was happening to the Palestinians. They didn't have proper health care or education; not even enough food. There was no end to the needs of the Palestinian people, the needs of my family, and even the size of my own career goals. In my culture we don't study just to improve ourselves; we study to raise the standard of living for our brothers and sisters. My family saw me as a role model, and goodness knows we were all in agreement about the need to improve the lives of Palestinians.

Nineteen eighty-three was also the year my brother Noor went missing; no one in my family has heard from him since then. The Israelis had put him in prison when he was eighteen years old because he was working for Fatah. Actually, I believe that he got caught up with a bad crowd of friends. He was discouraged, his self-esteem had faltered, and he had started dealing in hashish, although none of that was what got him arrested. When he got out of prison, he said he wanted to go back to Gaza or start over in Lebanon. He came to Cairo and stayed with me for six months. I told him I'd help him find work in one of the Gulf states, but in the end, he did not accept my offer and chose to go to Lebanon. The last time I saw him, he said, "I don't want to make trouble for you; leave me." I told him I couldn't leave him, that he was my brother, and that I would always love him and be responsible for him, but he went to Lebanon anyway. We could presume that he was killed and that no one has found his body, but we don't do that. If we don't know what happened, there is still hope. I think he would have been in touch if he was alive, but I push those thoughts aside. For me and my family, I maintain the hope that my eyes will see him again.

My return home was bittersweet. I had been offered a residency to become a specialist in obstetrics and gynecology in Cairo, but I turned it down, not only because I couldn't afford to stay on, but because my parents wanted me to come home.

My father was desperately ill with liver disease, and he had been hanging on, waiting for the moment when he would again see his son who had become a doctor, but his health was deteriorating daily. He had not been well enough to come to my graduation from medical school in Cairo. In fact the family stayed at home with him, so rather than have no one there to witness my graduation, I went home and missed it myself.

I was in for a shock when I got back to Gaza. I couldn't get a job in the place where I was born and raised; this place that was so much in need; the very place I had vowed to help by becoming a doctor. The Israelis had been occupying Gaza since 1967; it was now 1985. You could not travel anywhere in Gaza without seeing Israeli influence, and if you wanted to be employed, you had to be the son of an important person such as a government official or an influential person with connections to the Israelis, or a millionaire, or an Israeli collaborator.

Eventually, I was offered a position in the obstetrics and gynecology department at the Nasser hospital in Khan Yunis, nearly twenty-two miles away from Jabalia Camp; you couldn't get much farther from my home and still remain in the Gaza Strip. The position paid pocket money, so although I accepted it, I knew I would soon have to find something else.

Then, just eight months after I got home, my father died. Here was a man who had worked hard and suffered a lot. He was not familiar with rest and had to struggle for every piece of bread. He used to work day and night to save money for my education and living expenses in Cairo. He was employed at UNRWA as a simple worker from five or six in the morning until two in the afternoon. Then he would continue to work wherever anyone would hire him, either in Gaza or in Israel, from five in the evening until the next morning. He was waiting for his son to graduate from medical school. Sadly, though, my father did not get to reap this harvest from the seeds he had sown in his life. He had been a successful farmer, the son of a respected landowner, but then he was homeless, living in a refugee camp, raising his children there, working as a guard, never earning enough money. It was humiliating for him. I could feel his anxiety throughout my boyhood, and as my life began to improve at medical school in Cairo, I felt guilty that my father hadn't been able to be the role model to his children that he believed he should be. The last days of his life were painfully difficult. He had hepatic failure—his liver was shutting down. He was vomiting, he couldn't eat, and he was barely aware of his loving family hovering over him. When he slipped into a coma, we took him home, as there was nothing else the Al-Shifa hospital in Gaza City, where I was working, could do. As a doctor, I felt so helpless. I was the one who was supposed to help the patient, but this patient, my own father, could not be saved. I had vowed that once I graduated, my family would have a better home, enough to eat, and my father would know what he meant to me. I wanted him to see the fruits of his labor. I was going to be all that he'd been denied, but just as I was beginning to fulfill that promise, he was gone. I still feel the grief of his passing in my heart. So I will always do the three things that Muslims do for the dead: share his knowledge and wisdom with others, pray for him, and give to charity in his good name.

As for my career, I had been transferred from Nasser hospital in Khan Yunis to Al-Shifa hospital in Gaza, but this hospital, too, was not run by people with merit but by people with connections. A classmate from the university was the son of the director general of the department of health for the Gaza Strip.

His mother was chair of the obstetrics and gynecology department at Al-Shifa. He had gotten a job with an excellent salary even though he had been a playboy at the university and hadn't earned good marks. The next thing I knew, he was acting as though he was my superior, a big boss, always giving me orders.

So I quit and applied for a job with the Ministry of Health in Saudi Arabia. Actually, this was another of those cases where good came out of bad. I got the job, but it was almost 250 miles away, in Jeddah. I was not at all familiar with the place, and when my uncle said, "All those good times you had at school in Cairo are about to be paid back," I wondered if taking the job had been such a good idea. However, I had a close friend from medical school who was from Saudi Arabia, and I called him to find out how hard the posting and life in Jeddah would be. He was an ambassador's son, and so I too now had connections, and he got the perfect job for me, caring for Palestinians at Al-Aziziyah maternity ward. It wasn't Gaza, but it meant taking care of Palestinians, and it was an opportunity to test the waters of the medical specialty I had been drawn to from the time I studied obstetrics and gynecology at medical school.

The fact that I liked the job goes without saying, but this experience also gave me an opportunity to build a real social life and feel economic security for the first time. I earned enough to help my mother pay for repairs to our house in Jabalia; help my brother Atta go to the Philippines to study medicine, though he soon came back to Gaza and switched to pharmacy; and help another brother, Shehab, with money so he could get married. One of my half-brothers lived in Jeddah too, so we would get together at each other's houses. I enjoyed this kind of social life—being welcome in another house, talking, eating, sharing stories, having time to do things other than work, which was all I knew when I was growing up in Jabalia Camp. Then, just two years after starting the job, I had saved enough money to go back to Gaza and marry.

Nadia and I were married in Jabalia Camp in 1987. Only days after the celebration I had to return to Saudi Arabia by myself because she didn't have a visa and I couldn't apply for one until after we were married. She joined me about a month later. We lived in a rented house, and although we were unhappy about being so far away from our families, I did have my half-brother in Jeddah. I was happy to have relatives nearby; our culture places a high value on being near family.

Two months after our wedding, the first intifada began. Sadly, it started right in my neighborhood in Jabalia and spread pretty quickly throughout Gaza and into the West Bank and East Jerusalem. No one is really clear what triggered it. Some say it started because of an incident on December 8, 1987: an Israeli army tank ran into a group of Palestinians from Jabalia, killing four and injuring seven. A few days earlier, an Israeli salesman had been stabbed to death in Gaza, and many Palestinians felt the so-called accident was actually a revenge killing. Or it could have been retribution for another incident: a week before the intifada began, Palestinians had been accused of infiltrating an Israel Defense Forces (IDF) camp in Lebanon and killing six Israeli soldiers. Whatever the spark, people were outraged and took to the streets. The humiliation of the occupation knew no bounds; the Israeli soldiers would do stupid things like forcing a Palestinian to walk like a donkey just to make fun of him. Any small incident, real or imagined, could have set off the outrage, but as far as I could determine, the unrest came mostly from the fact that nothing was being done to alleviate the situation for Palestinians. There was no sign of establishing a Palestinian state; Palestinians needed an identity and citizenship. The leadership needed from the Arab states in order to resolve this issue was faltering. Palestinians had been waiting for change, for relief from intimidation and harassment, for twenty years since the Israelis took over in Gaza, and it was not surprising to see violence erupting in our streets.

At first it took the form of a lot of tire burning and stone throwing at Israeli troops. The response from the Israelis was disproportionate—kids throwing stones were met with soldiers attacking with M16 assault rifles. My brother Rezek was detained for no apparent reason. My sister had a miscarriage likely caused by the stress of the intifada. The daily news we were reading in Saudi Arabia was full of reports about attacks on the people and the deaths and injuries they suffered. The hostility was building every day: there were boycotts of Israeli goods, barricades were thrown up, there were strikes, and then Molotov cocktails and hand grenades were being thrown. It was not a good time to be away from home, as Nadia and I were always worried about what might happen next to our families and friends. On the other hand, soon enough Nadia was expecting, and personal joy and excitement battled for precedence in our hearts with these constant worries. Our daughter Bessan was born in July 1988.

In the personal realm, life was at last satisfying, even wonderful. I was gaining the medical experience I wanted. My family was growing and prospering, and despite my mother's desire to see me back home as the patriarch of the extended family, especially in these troubled times, I decided we would stay in Saudi Arabia for a while. A huge factor in this decision was that the opportunity to specialize in obstetrics and gynecology was presenting itself to me again, and this time I wanted to follow my dream. In early March 1988, I had received a scholarship from the Ministry of Health in Saudi Arabia to specialize in obstetrics and gynecology, getting my diploma at the Institute of Obstetrics and Gynecology at the University of London. I had become extremely interested in infertility. In Jabalia Camp there was a lot of infertility, which seems at odds with the high birth rates everyone assumes are the norm in Palestinian families. The paradox is that places with high fertility also turn out to have high infertility rates. I decided to do my thesis on this issue. Most of the classes were in Riyadh, the capital of Saudi Arabia, with only a few months of coursework in London.

I had a valid visa for travel to the United Kingdom, and my Palestinian passport caused me no travel problems; I boarded the plane for my first flight, brimming with excitement. I already spoke English, so I did not face much of a language barrier, and London was a larger-than-life experience for me. So different from Gaza—cold, rainy, dark—but alive, fascinating, cosmopolitan. It was a place where people from all over the world—all races, all religions—lived together, though of course I was aware of the conflict between the British and the IRA. The one thing that truly bothered me was the way the native-born British sometimes looked down on people who weren't British. I noticed that superior attitude on the street, in stores, and in community centers. Happily it didn't exist in the classroom, so it didn't affect my studies in London.

My research gave me a tempting taste of the work I could do in this field, and I was thoroughly smitten. I had seen so much suffering in women who were having difficulty conceiving. In a male-dominated culture such as my own, the woman is blamed for infertility problems even though not being able to produce a child can be the man's problem just as much as the woman's.

She is even blamed for the sex of the baby, although the Y chromosome that creates sons is an exclusively male factor in the conception process. I wanted men to know the facts and stop blaming the women, and I wanted those women to be relieved of the shame of being condemned as "barren." In my culture, ominous expressions such as "the unproductive tree should be cut" are common. I wanted to educate people so that they would never say such things about any woman again.

Working with couples who are trying to conceive, you learn how hard it is for them, how disappointed they are every single month that conception doesn't occur. But it's particularly painful for women, and I wanted to focus my efforts on how to alter that reality. As my research into infertility progressed and my clinical work in London and Jeddah with couples dealing with fertility problems started to produce excellent results, I decided to commit my career to this subspecialty. After I completed the course in 1989, I returned to Saudi Arabia and my job at Al-Aziziyah maternity ward. I was so glad to be reunited with my family. By then Nadia, who'd stayed in Jeddah to take care of Bessan and our second daughter, Dalal, who was born while I was in London, wanted to go home to Gaza. Saudi Arabia was much more conservative than Gaza; as Palestinians, we felt like foreigners there even though the Saudis were supposed to be our Arab brothers. I wasn't free to move where I wanted to move, and I worried that, as an outsider, I wouldn't advance much further than I'd already come in my career. The social norms were different; we found the restrictions too onerous. So we decided that we would leave, but it wasn't as easy as packing up the car and driving home. In order to repay the educational opportunities given to me by Saudi Arabia, I had to agree to provide three years of medical service. Only after that obligation was fulfilled could we go home.

Life was further complicated by the ever-present monsters in the Middle East: politics and war. The lead-up to the first Gulf War was creating problems for Palestinians in the Gulf states. In August 1990, Yasser Arafat made statements that sounded as though he approved of Saddam Hussein's invasion of Kuwait, and suddenly Palestinians were personae non gratae. I could see the writing on the wall: lots of Palestinians were being laid off in Saudi Arabia. Happily, by November 1990, my employers determined that I had fulfilled my obligations to the hospital in Jeddah, and Nadia and I were able to pack up our daughters and our belongings and return home on a bus. By the time the Gulf War began on January 16, 1991, my family and I were back in Gaza.

We arrived home in the midst of the continuing intifada. There were Israeli guns and tanks at every corner. Then, in the face of all this madness, it turned into a fratricidal bloodbath as well. An estimated one thousand Palestinians who were accused of collaborating with Israelis were executed by our own people, even though in most cases there was no proof of collusion. By the time the first intifada ended on August 20, 1993, with the signing of the Oslo Accords, more than 2,100 Palestinians were dead—1,000 at the hands of their own brothers and 1,100 killed by Israeli soldiers. One hundred and sixty Israelis had been killed by Palestinians. What came out of the intifada is hard to measure. Certainly the world began to pay attention to Palestinians as a result, and Israel got a black eye for its treatment of the Palestinians and for Palestinian living conditions. U.S. president Bill Clinton visited Gaza and Bethlehem in December 1998, becoming the first American president ever to visit any Palestinian territory and to deal directly with Palestinian leaders and institutions on their land. During the visit, Clinton made many important statements, coming very close to recognizing the Palestinian right to self-determination. He was accompanied by his family and by a large official delegation which included the secretary of state and the national security adviser. He then addressed a meeting in Gaza that was attended by Chairman Arafat, the speaker of the Palestinian National Council, the speaker of the Palestinian Council, members of the PNC, the Central Council, and the Palestinian Legislative Council, as well as by Palestinian heads of ministries and other personalities.

That the United States officially recognized the Palestine Liberation Organization as the legitimate representative of the Palestinian people was seen as a victory for us, but a new and disastrous weapon of terror was born during the intifada: suicide bombings. On April 16, 1993, in a parking lot at Mehola Junction, a rest area on the Jordan Valley Highway, a Palestinian man who had loaded his car with explosives drove it between two buses and detonated the bomb. The blast went upward instead of radiating out sideways, so most people were spared. A Palestinian who worked at the junction was killed, and so was the bomber. Twenty Israeli soldiers and civilians were injured. That horrible event began a string of equally terrible suicide bombings that paralyzed many regions of the Middle East with fear and led to the bloody destruction of our youths as well as the deaths of many innocents.

Certainly the people of Gaza, the West Bank, and Israel are not better off as a result of the birth of this inhumane tactic. Like the cost of most wars and uprisings, the cost in human treasure of the intifada and the suicide bombings was too high for everyone.

* * *

With money I had saved from my job in Saudi Arabia, I opened a private evening clinic in Gaza so that I could treat poor people in my own city. I was committed to providing care for people who could not afford it. I also accepted a post with the United Nations Relief and Works Agency as a field obstetrician and gynecologist. While studying at the University of London, I had noticed that most of the references I depended on for my thesis on infertility were by Israeli professors, so I decided to make a bold move and get in touch with the Israeli medical community to see what they were doing about infertility and to exchange ideas. Although the intifada continued apace, it didn't stop me from communicating with and eventually meeting my colleagues in Israel. I had come across an important textbook on infertility by two professors from Ben-Gurion University in Beersheba, Israel: Dr. Bruno Lunenfeld and Dr. Vaclav Insler. I called them, told them who I was and what I wanted, and was surprised when they were so willing to meet with me and provide advice on the care of my patients. In time, I started taking Palestinian patients to Dr. Lunenfeld's clinic. Some of them needed laparoscopic surgery, and he referred them to Marek Glezerman, who was at that time the chairman of the department of obstetrics and gynecology at Soroka hospital, in Beersheba. Because of the depth and importance of my subsequent relationship with Dr. Glezerman, I take the liberty of referring to him by his first name. Meeting Marek was a turning point in my career and my life. He immediately saw the value in bringing me onto his team and tried to figure out a way to make that happen. As I had no formal association with the doctors of Soroka hospital, he suggested I become a volunteer at the hospital to introduce myself to the Israeli medical system and to find out how its doctors were dealing with issues around obstetrics and gynecology, especially infertility. This was the new era of reproductive technologies, and I wanted to be at the cutting edge. I was hungry to learn, to expand my knowledge. My dream was to undertake a formal residency in obstetrics and gynecology, but it was a huge investment of time—four years—and there were finances to consider. For a long time I wondered if this particular dream was out of reach.

While I was moving back and forth between my UN position in Gaza and the volunteer work at Soroka, I was invited to attend the First World Congress on Labor and Delivery in Jerusalem in 1994. While I was in Jerusalem, I decided to try to find the Jewish family I had worked for as a teenager. I had been thinking about them for a long time but had never before tried to find their farm. Since I had to drive from Jerusalem back to Soroka, I decided this was the time to find the family who had had so much influence on me as a teenager; who had allowed me to see how small the differences actually were between the two peoples of the Middle East. I longed to show them that the Palestinian youth who had once worked for them was now a doctor and doing well. It was a reunion I'd imagined for a very long time. I knew they had lived near a village called Hodaia, somewhere along the road from Jerusalem to Beersheba. But where exactly was it? Could I find it again? The area had changed a lot, and the grandparents would be in their eighties by this time; I wondered if they were even alive.

I eventually found the farmhouse, and it was the granddaughter, who had been just a few days old when I left that summer, who opened the door. She asked what I needed. I answered, "I want to see your father." I had worked for her grandfather as well, but it was her father I knew best.

He was sitting on the couch near the window. He had noticed the Arab licence plates on the car when I turned into the driveway and had assumed I was an Arab businessman here to sell them something. He didn't recognize me at first. "You don't know me?" I asked. "I'll tell you who I am. I am Izzeldin, the one who worked here." With that, he jumped up from the couch and kissed and hugged me. When his wife saw me, she embraced me and said it felt as though she were holding her own son. She said, "Izzeldin, I remember you, the boy who worked in the chicken coops and was always holding his nose because he could not bear the smell. I used to pity you and think it's not a place for a youngster to work."

I was so happy to have found the family once again and to see that they were all alive and well. I was glad to have the chance to explain to them how much my summer at their farm had meant to me: that it had proved to me that Jews and Palestinians could behave as one family. They told me that they had never expected that a doctor would come out of a place like the Jabalia refugee camp, a place full of fighting and hostility. I wanted to show them the affection, even love, I had for them. I know how much we can accomplish when we pull down the barriers that stop us from achieving our dreams.

Back at Soroka hospital, my Israeli colleagues kept talking to me about taking up a residency there in obstetrics and gynecology. I simply couldn't see how to do it. I was still running my clinic in Gaza, earning enough money for the family, and coming regularly to Soroka to consult with and learn from my new colleagues.

Marek Glezerman tailored the program to suit me and recommended that I be the first Palestinian resident in his department, but left for a position at another hospital before he could follow through. He was replaced by a new chair, Moshe Mazor, who also supported the idea, but it wasn't easy. For example, the hospital had to arrange for four different certificates just to get me started. I had to carry a special identification card as well as a work permit that was good for one year, a license giving me permission to sleep in Israel on nights when I couldn't make it home, and a special license that allowed me to cross the border in my own car (we could drive cars across the border then). Shimon Glick and Margalith Carmi, both professors at Ben-Gurion University's school of medicine, were crucial, persuading the MacArthur Foundation to establish a grant to cover my salary.

Dr. Shlomo Usef, who became the director of Soroka at that time, was also supportive. He said, "Izzeldin was a special person, with a balanced point of view about the Israeli-Palestinian conflict . . . He saw it as a conflict with two sides, and himself as the person to bridge the two. On top of that, he had aspirations to reach new heights in his own work. So I thought we should train him. We had to deal with everything—his career, the finances required, all the permits he would need from our government and his to make this happen. We did it all through Ben-Gurion University. I saw how eager Izzeldin was to move ahead. So I wanted to help to make sure his residency at Soroka began. The rest he did on his own."

I took up the residency in 1997, almost exactly one year after our first son, Mohammed, was born. Nadia was now at home with him and our five older daughters. I know it was difficult for her. I was away during the week, and often on weekends as well if I was scheduled to work a shift at the hospital. The border crossing between Gaza and Israel was so unpredictable I never knew if I could get across in time to be at work, so I rented a small apartment in Beersheba and used part of the two-thousand-dollar monthly salary I was being paid to cover these expenses. Otherwise I was worried I'd be late for a class or to relieve another resident at the end of a shift or for a patient who was depending on me. Even though I got to know many of the soldiers and they didn't hassle me, the new ones or the ones I didn't know gave me no end of grief, just as they did with other Palestinians coming into Israel. I was learning, yes, but I was also serving the Israeli patients in the hospital—it was not an easy situation.

One time, I was asked to drive my car over the pit where soldiers inspected the undersides of cars. I sat at the side with my briefcase, watching the process, trying to be patient. When at last the screening was finished, I drove away. It wasn't until I reached the hospital that I realized I'd left my briefcase with my license, my passport, all of my documents and important papers on the landing beside the car. I phoned the crossing station, but there was no answer. So I drove the twenty-seven miles back to the crossing and told the soldiers about my dilemma. The man in charge hardly even raised his head to look at me. He said, "We thought it was a suspicious package, and we blew it up."

I understood the security issue. They wouldn't take the risk. Security is as important for Palestinians as it is for Israelis. But those soldiers knew me, and they ought to have dealt with me not as a Palestinian but as a human being. I was simply a man who had forgotten his briefcase. There are plenty of Palestinians who are also looking for peace, and they deserve the same respect as anyone else at the crossing. Still, I put up with the indignity because I did not want to jeopardize my chance to learn at Soroka hospital. It took two months to replace the documents that had been destroyed.

*   *   *

My research was in the fertility unit. My patients were Israeli and Palestinian and Arab-Israeli couples who were having difficulty conceiving a child. The department was like a world unto itself and transcended the two worlds.

Life in general is not easy, not for anyone, but it is especially difficult for couples who are dealing with infertility, with all its additional baggage of anguish and self-doubt. Somehow this pain has always resonated with me: from the beginning of my training, I have always wanted to help relieve this fundamental ache in men and women who want to become parents and yet cannot conceive. It is the reason why work in this field continues to be so important to me.

However, there were—and still are—so many unique challenges in the way of our finding the path to peaceful coexistence. For instance, a critically ill woman from Gaza was brought in for treatment; she would have died had she stayed in Gaza. She was a mother of ten with acute renal failure, and she had been in a Gaza hospital for about two weeks, with the diagnosis of deep-vein thrombosis and marked swelling in her legs. But then she developed a high fever and other complications, and a decision was made to transfer her to Soroka. It's not easy to move patients across this divide. A Palestinian ambulance had to bring her to the Erez Crossing. An ambulance from Soroka had to meet her there and make the switch. It was (and still is) difficult to get permission to cross into Israel. Not only that, but the Palestinian Authority had to agree to pay her medical costs before she could leave. There was a lot of distrust between Palestinians and Israelis at that time, as there still is, and as a consequence so much needless suffering, pain, and loss on both sides. Nevertheless, a transfer was coordinated, and she was moved to Soroka. I was consulted when she got there to determine if there was a gynecological reason for the high fever. When I spoke to her in Arabic and told her I was a Palestinian from Jabalia Camp, she grabbed my hand and wouldn't let go. She had never been to Israel before and was afraid she'd be mistreated. But it was Israeli doctors who saved her life. I love my work because a hospital is a place where humanity can be discovered, where people are treated without racism and as equals. In the brotherhood and sisterhood of medicine, we take an oath to care for the sick when we graduate. Whether it is the Hippocratic Oath, the Prayer of Maimonides, or the Declaration of Geneva, no matter where in the world we graduate or what language we speak, we leave our differences outside those walls and we are dedicated to saving lives. Certainly I cannot speak for everyone, but in my experience the Israelis I worked with see the patient, not the nationality or the ethnicity.

There is another experience from my days at Soroka hospital I would like to describe. I was determined to learn Hebrew, because I never wanted a patient to think I couldn't read his or her chart or understand the symptoms; I was afraid that he or she would lose confidence in my work if my command of the language was insufficient. So I was very careful to speak grammatically correct Hebrew. One day a Bedouin woman was admitted with severe hypertension in her pregnancy, but she refused to stay in the hospital. I had to write a discharge summary and record the fact that she had refused medical advice. In Hebrew the word for "refused" is *mesarevet*. I didn't know the symbol for the letter *s*—whether it went one way or the other—and I didn't want the Bedouin woman or her husband to know that in case they'd wonder why the doctor couldn't spell. For that reason, I couldn't ask the nurse how to spell this word in front of the patient. Believe it or not, for that reason alone, I tried to persuade the patient to stay in the hospital. She wouldn't. Finally I asked her to go with her husband to his car and bring her identification to me, just so I could get them out of the room long enough to ask the nurse how to make an *s* in Hebrew. When the couple came back and I asked them to sign the discharge sheet, they told me neither of them could write their names.

I had been so worried about making a mistake in front of them. I was always aware that I could be judged as lacking, whether it be in medical skill or language or interpersonal relationships. As much as I'd been given the opportunity of a lifetime to be a resident at Soroka, I knew I was a test case in the eyes of my Israeli colleagues, and that my success could create openings for other Palestinian physicians in the future. My failure might shut that door.

Most Jewish Israelis mistook me for an Arab-Israeli, but I quickly told them I was a Palestinian from the Gaza Strip. Although I wore a name tag with a Palestinian surname and spoke Hebrew with an accent, no one seemed to object. Disease doesn't recognize borders. But I have to admit, politics and prejudice keep pushing their way into things. I just wanted to do my job at the hospital and leave the politics at the checkpoint, but they came right with me into the emergency room. For example, one afternoon at about four o'clock I was in the gynecology department's emergency room when a woman arrived in distress. She was in the early stages of pregnancy and was bleeding. I examined her, did an ultrasound, found that the pregnancy was intact but that she was at risk for miscarriage. The only treatment was bed rest. I told her there was only a fifty-fifty chance the pregnancy could be saved.

She left the hospital but came back at midnight; the bleeding had increased. This time her husband, a Sephardic Jew from Morocco, started shouting at me, claiming I killed the baby and threatening to do the same to me. I was busy dealing with the patient—his wife. He continued threatening me, and the nurse called for security. This man would not have treated an Israeli doctor like this. He blamed me for his wife's condition because he saw me first and foremost as an Arab. He complained to the head of the hospital, who took the man to his office, pointed at the shelves full of medical textbooks, and said, "What Dr. Abuelaish did came from these textbooks." He defended me wholeheartedly, and the man calmed down.

I did my share of pushing the envelope for coexistence even then by acting as an unofficial peace envoy for the region: I would host groups of Israelis at my home or in the homes of my friends one weekend every month. We toured the Jabalia refugee camp and Gaza City, showed them the conditions people live in, let them experience the overcrowding, and allowed plenty of time so they could talk to people, ask their own questions, and draw their own conclusions. Then we'd have coffee and sweets together—all of us, the Israelis and the Palestinians. We'd discuss, and we'd argue. These get-togethers brought home to me how similar we are when it comes to socializing. We're expressive. We talk loudly, and the decibel level goes up with the intensity of the conversation. The more interesting it gets, the noisier we become. That's how Palestinians and Israelis are. But I can say that even the most vociferous arguments almost always ended with the exchange of telephone numbers and the forging of friendships.

Then it stopped. The second intifada began in September 2000 when a number of incendiary events came together like a forest fire. Ariel Sharon visited the Temple Mount, the third most holy site in the Islamic world, in a show of "I dare you to try to stop me." The peace talks at the Camp David Summit in July had collapsed; skirmishes on both sides had resulted in deaths. Then the rock throwing, the firebombing, and the tear-gassing began. Riots followed. The border was closed, and my little band of peacemakers were no longer allowed to meet.

I continued working in my own clinic in Gaza one day a week, giving medical treatment for free. But even I couldn't cross into Israel during the first several weeks, and the approximately one hundred thousand other Gazans who had jobs in Israel couldn't go to work either. It felt as though we were being squeezed out of existence. No jobs and no money means no food and no goods. Although it would get a lot worse later, many Palestinians couldn't see any future for themselves. They began to see their lives as useless. And then, when one person goes crazy and becomes a suicide bomber, no one around him tries to prevent the act. Instead, they call him a hero. That's the way things get worse.

I wanted to go back to work in Israel, and in order to protect myself, I consulted many Palestinians about whether or not I should. I wanted to know if it was ethical. The general consensus was, "Izzeldin, go to your work. It's beneficial for you, for us, for the Israelis." I still had the papers that allowed me to cross into Israel, and despite the fact that the intifada was still raging, it was business as usual when I presented them at the border.

When I arrived back at the genetic institute at Soroka hospital for the first time after a sixty-day absence, my Israeli colleagues and friends accepted me like a son who had come home after much too long. They told me they had all been thinking of me, and Dr. Ohad Burke, director of the genetic institute, welcomed me back with flowers and a big hug. One of my Israeli friends at Soroka told me, "Izzeldin, I heard that you were afraid to come back. I want to tell you I am ready to sacrifice my life for your safety if any Israeli tries to do harm to you." What more can anyone do than this?

But even after my preemptive consultations, some of my colleagues in Gaza questioned my motives. One said, "How can you help these Jewish women to have babies? They will grow up to be soldiers who bomb us and shoot us." Another said through clenched teeth, "It makes me very angry that you are doing this." Some suggested I was helping to deliver a new generation of occupiers. I tried to tell them that these Israeli babies could grow up to be doctors.

I felt as if we'd been so close to peace. Like many others, I had been full of hope. I'd been conducting my tours and had even opened other clinics in Gaza with the help of Israeli doctors (which all had to close). I find it astonishing that the two sides could be so close to a peace agreement and then see their relationship deteriorate so rapidly. As the second intifada raged, each side was focusing on its own pain and blaming the other instead of realizing we have to recognize the rights of both peoples to live in harmony and peace; the alternative is war and distrust. I wished then that I could close my eyes and open them to where we had been before the second intifada began, when we were still talking to each other.

I walked a fine line while trying to bring together the two sides of a very fractious debate. I thought that attracting more Palestinian doctors to Israeli hospitals to do their residencies would show them the real Israelis who believe in peace, and it would also allow Israelis to see the human aspect of the

Palestinian. Politics aside, I believe the best way to bring peace between our two peoples is through health care. For me, every patient is like one of my relatives. I don't make any distinction: Israeli, Palestinian, Arab-Israeli, new immigrant, Bedouin. My duty is to make sure every child has the same chance for health at birth. But look what happens after these innocent children grow up. Who is telling them these things that turn them into enemies rather than friends?

The second intifada actually proved more than anything else how much we Palestinians and Israelis are stuck with one another, and that we have to find a way to live together. The failure in the peace process was a failure for both sides. We were both linked to it, and because we couldn't find détente, we ended up with another intifada.

Though the conflict kept raging, my brothers and I decided to build a new house—a five-story building where we could live separately but together, one brother on each floor except for the first floor, which we reserved for our mother. We chipped in together, although I paid for most of it, and constructed a house in Jabalia City, on the outskirts of the camp. My brother Shehab lived nearby, while my three sisters lived with their husbands and their husbands' relatives in Jabalia Camp and Gaza City. But like everything else in our lives, the new house presented a new dilemma. Our mother, Dalal, the strongest woman I'd ever known, refused to move in with us. She was still waiting for my brother Noor to come home. All those years, she hung up his shirts to air and pressed his trousers, hoping that he would walk through the door and all would be as it was. She watched constantly for him. She wouldn't leave the small house in the refugee camp that had been built with the money I earned at fifteen in case Noor came home and couldn't find us. Of course, everyone knew where we were now, and they would have told him how to find us. But our mother stood her ground and would not set foot in our lovely new home when we moved there in September 2001. So each of her sons took turns staying with her. One of my brothers named his daughter Noor and another named his son Noor. We kept him in the family that way. It's all we could do. My mother regularly dreamed that she saw him returning home, though he had been gone for eighteen years.

I was on duty on September 11, 2001, in the emergency room of the gynecology department at Soroka hospital. We were busy with patients that night, so busy I hardly had time to scratch my head. At about midnight one of the cleaners said, "Buildings are falling in America." I went to a room with a television and saw what he was talking about. The first tower of the World Trade Center was collapsing. Nobody thought terror could come to the United States. But it had.

As a Palestinian, I knew a thing or two about terror. I had been living with it for much of my life. Soon after the tragedy of 9/11, I was invited to participate in a panel discussion at a symposium the American Friends of Soroka Medical Center of the Negev were organizing in New York City. It was titled "After Terrorism Strikes: A Dialogue of Healing." The other panelists were the journalist David Makovsky, a senior fellow at the Washington Institute for Near East Policy; the lawyer Steven Flatow, the father of Alisa Flatow, who was killed by a suicide bomber in Gaza; and Esther Chachkes, the director of the social work department at New York University Medical Center. I knew immediately that I wanted to accept this invitation, wanted to address this audience on this topic. But then I heard from the organizer, Mona Abramson, my friend and colleague of five years at Soroka hospital, that one of the other panelists wanted my name withdrawn.

It was Steven Flatow who rejected my name. He had asked Mona, "What's a Palestinian from Gaza coming to this conference for? My daughter was killed in Gaza." But Abramson told me that she persuaded him by saying, "Don't be judgmental, don't be impulsive, and don't say no without knowing." When Mona explained the resistance to me and asked if I'd still be a panelist, I told her I was ready, that I didn't even have to think twice about this opportunity because that's the way I saw it: as an opportunity to cross this bridge to get to the Jewish community. This is precisely where the healing needed to begin. I carefully prepared my message, wanting to make every single word count. I wasn't nervous, but I was upset because I realized that they could only see themselves and didn't want to see me or understand what I needed to tell them.

I flew to New York determined to speak my truth, but began to worry about what I'd face as the only Palestinian voice on the panel. When I got there, it was clear that the audience was mostly Jewish. Even before the panel discussion began, members of the audience were tossing provocative comments my way. One said, "You raise your kids to hate us." I wanted to let them know what life was really like for Palestinians, and I felt the gravitas of the situation because it was an opportunity to open their eyes. As baseball fans right here in America would say, "I had to hit this speech out of the park" if I wanted to change their view of Palestinians. I looked at the audience in front of me and understood the size of the task before me. You can tell when people have closed minds—they lean back in their chairs, don't make eye contact, and behave as though their attendance is a perfunctory task. Maybe they were only here to see the other panelists put me in my place; that happens as well, but it usually doesn't end that way. I had information they didn't have, I had the stories to tell, and I had a case to make. I reminded myself to smile when it was my turn to speak. There were about three hundred people in the room. I was the third speaker. They'd already heard from Steven Flatow when I stepped up to the podium. At first I wondered if they were even able to hear me, given the size of the terrorist tragedy they had just suffered. Could they process the agony of another when they'd just been attacked themselves? I wanted to tell them about the last four weeks in the Middle East, about the extreme tension between Israelis and Palestinians, about Ariel Sharon saying, "Everyone has his Osama bin Laden; ours is Yasser Arafat," about the blameless Palestinian children who had been killed, the people on both sides, including leaders, who'd been assassinated in brutal acts of revenge, the lynching of Israeli soldiers in Ramallah, the anti-Arab pogrom in Nazareth. September 11 had unleashed a toll on my side of the world as well. That's how terrorism establishes its roots. By finding its way among the disenfranchised, the discontented, and the uneducated, it germinates fear, distrust, and intolerance.

I didn't want to talk about Balfour Declarations and peace accords and Jewish settlements and smugglers' tunnels between Gaza and Egypt. Everyone talks about those issues incessantly, to the extent that it is the only daily subject of conversation. Isn't there anything else? I know it's everywhere; it's embedded in every fiber of their being. They speak, eat, drink, and sleep this political issue. Still, I wanted so much to shift the focus, to talk about people, about trust, respect, and tolerance. I wanted to share what I knew of Israelis and Palestinians, how much alike we are.

We all need to understand that there are evil people in every country, every religion, every culture. But there is also a silent camp of people in every country who believe, like I do, that we can bring two communities together by listening to each other's points of view and concerns. It's that simple. I know it is; I've been doing it for almost all of my adult life. Look at the Middle East, the bruised Holy Land, and its generations of hatred and bloodshed. The way to replace that is with dialogue and understanding. Trust in the Middle East is such a rare commodity today; it's gasping for air. The thing is, you cannot ask people to coexist by having one side bow their heads and rely on a solution that is only good for the other side. What you can do is stop blaming each other and engage in dialogue with one person at a time. Everyone knows that violence begets violence and breeds more hatred. We need to find our way together. I feel I cannot rely on the various spokespersons who claim they act on my behalf. Invariably they have some agenda that doesn't work for me. Instead, I talk to my patients, to my neighbors and colleagues—Jews, Arabs—and I find out they feel as I do: we are more similar than we are different, and we are all fed up with the violence.

As a physician who has practiced in Israel and Gaza, I see medicine as the bridge between us, just as education and friendship have been bridges. We all know what to do, so who is stopping us? Who is holding up the barrier between our two sides? We need to reach each other by embracing one another's realities, sending messages of tolerance rather than intolerance and healing instead of hate.

I watched this audience of Jewish Americans while I spoke. I could see them absorbing the truth when I recited the facts of life in Gaza. They weren't leaning back in their chairs waiting for me to finish. Like decent people everywhere, they were shocked by what I had to say and a little surprised by the simplicity of my message. I knew I had scored when Steven Flatow, the man who didn't approve of my presence on the panel, stood up and said, "Tomorrow you are invited for Shabbat lunch at my house." He sent a limousine for me the next day. We had lunch with his mother, and after lunch he said, "Izzeldin, what can I do for the Gazans?" There was no better gift I could have received that day.

In February 2002, my mother died, and I felt I had lost the person who sacrificed the most for me. She was the one who held the family together when I was a child. It was her strength—sometimes outright bullying—that moved all of us forward. Just a few days before she died, I found her standing on the street waiting for a ride to her cousin's house, and I took her there in my car. She seemed much as she had always been, strong and healthy.

We had just celebrated Eid's Feast of Sacrifice; my mother was euphoric at seeing her children and grandchildren together. I was heading home afterward to pack for a trip I was supposed to make to San Francisco to attend a meeting on behalf of the hospital, and just as I got in the door, my brother called to tell me my mother was not well. When I got back to her house, I realized that she had had a stroke, and I got her into my car to take her to Al-Shifa hospital in Gaza. After she was admitted to the intensive care unit, I called Soroka to say I couldn't make the trip, and my colleagues suggested I bring her there. I considered the offer because Al-Shifa didn't always have the equipment patients needed, but when I went to see her in the hospital that day, I found the minister of health for the Palestinian Authority making an official visit to the hospital and a flurry of officials attending him. He stopped by my mother's room to say hello to me, and after his visit the staff made sure my mother had everything she needed. At Al-Shifa, it's still about who you know. As a physician, I realized the best we could do was to keep my mother comfortable. As a son, I made sure that when she regained consciousness and asked for Bessan, who had spent many nights with her grandmother over the years, that I brought Bessan to see her. The whole family stayed at her bedside day and night until she passed away three days later.

I felt so sad to lose this woman. I had wanted to give her a better life, take care of her, make up for the hardship she had suffered. Somehow I always felt it was never enough. She would have been so proud of me graduating from the residency program at Soroka and becoming the first Palestinian doctor on staff in an Israeli hospital, but that was still a few months away. When we took her body to the cemetery to be buried, the funeral cortège drove by the new house my brothers and I had built. That's as close as she ever got to it.

A month after my mother died, there was a suicide bombing at a hotel in Israel. Although I was on the other side of the country and obviously had nothing to do with the plan, I was immediately barred from entering Israel, prevented from seeing my patients, from doing my job. It took two months and intervention from many Israeli colleagues from the hospital, and even members of the Knesset, the Israeli parliament, to overturn the prohibition and allow me as an individual to cross the border again. People often tell me they admire my patience and ability to be calm and avoid rash and impulsive behavior. I tell them I learned all of it while waiting in line at the Erez checkpoint.

The next year, our second son, Abdullah, was born. Our family was complete. Patient man or not, as I made my way through the border to and from work, I wondered what kind of a world this family of mine was growing up in.

Depending on whom you listen to, the second intifada ended in November 2004, when Yasser Arafat died, or in February 2005, when Mahmoud Abbas agreed to stop the violence and Israel's Sharon agreed to release nine hundred Palestinian prisoners. But who knows when or even if it ended. Until people start to talk to each other, this problem is not going to go away.

In those years, I was away from home a lot. As soon as I completed my residency, I was sponsored by the American Friends of Ben-Gurion University and the American Friends of Soroka to receive specialist training in fetal medicine and genetics at V. Buzzi hospital in Milan, Italy, and Erasme hospital in Brussels, Belgium. My dreams to be an expert in obstetrics and gynecology were coming true.

Such travel also opened my eyes to the huge need for better public health policies, particularly among populations such as the Palestinians. A friend of mine organized a meeting for me in Boston with the dean of academic affairs of Harvard University's School of Public Health, and the dean told me, "You can benefit from us, and we can benefit from you." What he meant, of course, was that I had firsthand experience with the public health issues in an overcrowded refugee camp, and he had expertise in how to create public health policy; together, we could innovate the theory around public health policy. But studying in Boston would mean another long period away from home. I also wasn't sure I was in the right frame of mind for writing another set of exams, this time the Graduate Record

Examination for entrance to Harvard. I had been studying for exams for decades. I wanted to get back to the business of building a career. Still, the public health issue and health policy and management skills kept calling me; I knew they were like missing puzzle pieces for the work I wanted to do and the skills I wanted to acquire in the medical field. Eventually I made the decision to accept the scholarship Harvard was offering and left in 2003 to do the twelve-month master's degree in health policy and management.

The experience turned out to be invaluable, exposing me to a whole different realm of the medical world and making me aware of opportunities for improving the health care of Palestinians. The health system in the Gaza Strip is fragmented; services are duplicated and poorly coordinated, so they don't meet the needs of the people. The United Nations still covers primary health care; the Palestinian Authority does the rest. But too many people are caught in the middle. If you have a simple disease, it's okay, but if you have a serious problem, you need to go outside Gaza to be treated. Obviously this has an impact on the health of the people. The bottom line is that every time the administration changes, the health system undergoes a metamorphosis that's dependent on the people in charge rather than the needs of the population. I wanted to find a way to reverse those facts. The downside was that, because I was traveling on a student visa to the United States, I couldn't go back to Gaza to visit. The rules of the visa were so strict that if I had come home to visit my family, even over the lengthy Christmas holiday break at Harvard, I would not have been able to return to complete my studies. So I lived in Boston for the whole academic year, and although I missed my family, I focused on studying. I also enjoyed the friends I made there.

There were students from all over the world who had a myriad of experiences with their medical practices and an enormous amount of information to share. I confess I had come to the United States under the impression that Americans are arrogant people. Living among them taught me not to judge people by the frustrations you may have with their government. This was an open, competitive society that was built on concepts of success. My time in Boston taught me that most Americans are kind people and good neighbors. Judging them all as arrogant is the same as calling all Israelis occupiers and all Palestinians troublemakers.

Even in those democratic, human rights–conscious classes at Harvard, though, the old Middle East issues still came up. When I was selecting a class for health economics, there were two professors who taught the course I needed; one of them was a Jew. A classmate from the United Arab Emirates told me to study with the other professor because he said the Jewish one hated Arabs. I signed up for the class with the Jewish professor anyway because he was known as an expert in the field of health economics and I wanted to learn from the best, but I did get the impression that he was ignoring me in class. Was that my own paranoia after being warned about him, or was he really isolating me from the other students?

I decided to ask for a private meeting. When I went in to see him, I was absolutely straightforward. I said, "You know I am a Palestinian. I know you are a Jew. I was told not to take this class because you wouldn't treat me fairly. It feels as though you are ignoring me in class, and I want to ask you if this is true." He was flabbergasted. He said he had no idea I felt neglected in his class. We talked about it, and as I tried to offer examples that would justify my concerns, I realized they were petty and insignificant and that I had been influenced by my classmate who had advised against taking the course with this professor. I felt foolish after that and wondered even then if he would hold it against me. But he didn't. In fact a few weeks after that meeting he stopped me after class to say there was a speaker coming from the World Bank and that he wanted me to meet her.

I graduated on June 10, 2004, and was back in Gaza by June 12. I wished my family could have been there at the commencement. I wished my mother and father could have risen from their graves to see me, their son, a boy of poverty, accepting my degree. I wanted all Palestinians to share the moment with me, but it wasn't possible. The faculty raised the flag of the country of every graduating student in the commencement ceremony, and when I saw the flag of Palestine up there with the others, I was proud of who I am and who we are together.

My homecoming was bittersweet. I had been away so long, the children felt estranged from me. My son Abdullah, who was only a year old when I left, didn't even know me. He heard his cousins calling me uncle and called me uncle as well. I had three suitcases full of gifts for the children, including a black wool coat for Bessan that cost more than I had ever paid for anything before, dresses for my other daughters, and American toys for the younger children. Sadly, my three eldest daughters weren't there. Bessan, Dalal, and Shatha were away at the peace camp in Santa Fe, New Mexico. I had to wait another two long weeks before seeing them. My brothers and their families were there, and so was most of the neighborhood. We talked and laughed and ate my favorite food, which Nadia had prepared. There was noise and fun and celebrations for about two weeks. It felt awfully good to be home.

FOUR

Hearts and Minds

So much of what happens in my homeland results from decisions made a long way from the streets of Jabalia City. The Oslo Accords, signed in 1993, called for the Gaza Strip to be part of the Palestinian Authority, along with the West Bank; a potential corridor connecting the two would eventually form a Palestinian state. Yasser Arafat was the leader of both regions, and the two main political parties, Hamas and Fatah, vied for the loyalties of Palestinians. Fatah was more dominant in the West Bank. Hamas, a Palestinian Islamic sociopolitical movement, headquartered in Gaza and founded in 1987 by Sheikh Ahmed Yassin as an offshoot of Egypt's Muslim Brotherhood, preached an ideology based on Palestinian nationalism, Islamism, and religious nationalism. Like Fatah, its name comes from an acronym of the Arabic words that make up the full name of the organization: Islamic Resistance Movement. Hamas got most of its support from Gazans, and it was Hamas that launched the suicide bombings in April 1993 (and only renounced them in April 2006).

In September 2005, Israeli settlers were withdrawn from Gaza, fulfilling a promise from the Israeli government that the territory would be controlled by Palestinians. It wasn't exactly a success story. Israel acted unilaterally and the border crossings were still controlled by Israelis, but it was an important step forward all the same. At least, that's the way I saw it. The withdrawal from Gaza was one of those momentous events that make political head-lines around the world, but on the ground there are other scenes acted out on an almost daily basis that are largely ignored by the international media yet play relentlessly on the hearts and minds of the Gazan and Israeli peoples. I've been involved with some of these, whether I wanted to be or not.

For example, a couple of months before the Israeli settlers withdrew, on June 21, 2005, a woman from my home in Jabalia tried to attack the hospital where I was working. Her name was Wafa Samir Ibrahim al-Biss, a twenty-one-year-old Palestinian, and she had actually been a patient at the hospital after she had suffered burns in a cooking accident. After her release, she was issued an outpatient card and a special pass that allowed her to cross into Israel to receive the ongoing treatment she needed. No one was more surprised than I was to learn what happened next. On her way to the hospital, she was stopped at the Erez Crossing because an alert security guard became suspicious. It turned out that she had ten pounds of explosives strapped to her hips. Her plan was to detonate herself in the hospital, and she later admitted that she had intended to take out as many people as she could, even children.

I was so outraged that I wrote an open letter to the *Jerusalem Post*, published on June 24, expressing my disgust with her actions and my solidarity with the hospital. After expressing my dismay, I wrote: "On the very day she planned to detonate her bomb, two Palestinians in critical condition were waiting in Gaza to be taken for urgent medical treatment to Soroka." There are several militant factions that mastermind these atro-cious acts; whoever it was who sent Biss, they wanted her to kill the very people in Israel who are healing Palestinians from the Gaza Strip and West Bank. What if Israeli hospitals now decide to bar Palestinians seeking treatment? How would those who sent this young woman feel if their own relatives, in need of medical care in Israel, were refused treatment?

My open letter continued: "As for Biss herself, she should have been a messenger for peace among her people, and should have been bringing flowers and appreciation to the Soroka doctors for healing her burns . . . To plan an operation of this kind against a hospital is an act of evil. Children, women, patients, doctors and nurses were the target. Is this a reward for kindness? Is this an advertisement for Islam, a religion which respects and sanctifies human life? This is aggression and a violation of humanity."

I assumed she had been brainwashed; otherwise how could she turn on the people who had helped her? I know the Gazans were pleased that I wrote the letter; they said it spoke for them. Even some politicians, who felt they couldn't get involved publicly, told me that I'd said what they were unable to say. As for Wafa al-Biss, she's in an Israeli prison, and I doubt she will be getting out anytime soon.

During my time at Harvard University, the thought of entering politics began to poke its way into my consciousness. I had always rejected the political arena, had felt certain it wasn't the way I could make a contribution to my people. But as I studied health policy and realized how much a well-thought-out plan with carefully created policies could move the Palestinian people out of their chaos and deprivation, I was drawn like the proverbial moth to the flame. There was an upcoming political election in Gaza, and when I got home, I began immediately to test the waters for a possible run for office in the Palestinian Legislative Council. For months I went to every single community event in

Me at twenty-two.

Deep in my medical studies in Cairo.

I am to the left of my father. Behind us are my brothers Shehab and Nasser, and on the other side of my father is my older half-brother Ahmad.

ALL IMAGES ARE COURTESY OF THE AUTHOR.

From left, my brother Noor, who went missing in 1983 after a stint in an Israeli jail, and my siblings Rezek, Etimad, Atta, and Shehab.

My mother, Dalal, was a lioness when it came to protecting us, but she was demanding as well.

With Nadia at our wedding.

Nadia with our firstborn,
Bessan, in our home
in Saudi Arabia.

At the beach in happier
times, in 2004, after I
got back from Harvard.
Five of our children:
from left, Mohammed,
Aya, Dalal, Bessan, and
Abdullah in the arms of
his mother, Nadia.

From left, Mayar, my
niece Etimad, Bessan,
Shatha, Abdullah, Aya,
Raffah, and Dalal.

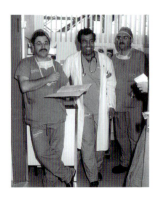

With Israeli colleagues who
worked with me in the
in vitro fertilization unit at
Soroka hospital.

In 2001, meeting with the Israeli minister of
health, Yehoshua Matza (right), who was surprised
to encounter a Palestinian doctor in an Israeli
hospital.

Meeting Israeli prime
minister Ehud Barak
(far left) with his first
wife, Nava, in 2001.

One of my earlier attempts
to bridge the distance
between Israel and the
Gaza Strip. I arranged
for Yaakov Terner (right),
the mayor of Beersheba
and former police chief,
to come to police head-
quarters in Gaza to meet
the Palestinian police
chief, Ghazi al-Jabali.
After Hamas won the
election in 2006, all such
efforts had to stop.

The apartment building I
built with my brothers in Jabalia
City to house our families.
The photo was taken a year after
the shelling.

My niece Noor, who died
with my three daughters on
January 16, 2009.

Aya wanted to be a journalist when she grew up, and was the poet in the family.

Mayar was the top math student in her school in grade nine, and wanted to become a doctor like me.

Bessan, at twenty-one, had almost completed her business degree; she took on a mother's role with her younger siblings after Nadia died.

My daughters' bedroom after the shelling.

Their grave in the Gaza Strip, on the anniversary of the girls' death, January 16, 2010.

There is no caption that can express a father's loss.

the northern part of the Gaza Strip. My message was "I am here for you. I am going to make changes that will affect health and education in Gaza."

Since the election was still months off, I took a job working as the reproductive health consultant at the Maram Project, a small program the Palestinian Authority was running with a donation from USAID. Since the work took me all over the Gaza Strip, I was also able to continue to talk about my plan to run in the upcoming election. I believed that I was received very well; people on the streets were saying, "He's back. He's going to be in the government." I was also giving lectures at Soroka hospital and doing medical referrals from my own home. So I was in a good position to develop community relationships and to let people know that I had a plan.

I told my neighbors that I knew what was wrong and I knew how to fix it. The health system—from its administration to its performance—was inadequate. Progress was determined only by who had the power to hand out jobs rather than by the needs of the people. By now I had international experience in London, Belgium, and Italy, as well as at Harvard University. I had worked for the United Nations and been on the staff of a number of different hospitals in Gaza, Israel, and Saudi Arabia. I had seen the way good health systems operate, and I knew how to bring them to Gaza. Furthermore, I had established relationships with doctors and administrators in all these international centers, and I knew I could count on them to help me.

Conditions in Gaza had deteriorated sharply while I had been at Harvard, and I knew that we needed new blood very badly on the political front. Although I had been abroad for two years and needed to reestablish myself, I believed that the people wanted the changes I was proposing.

Basically, I campaigned for the rest of 2005. My brothers helped me, and friends did too. We all thought my chances for success were good. Some asked how I could forgo the money I would make as a doctor to campaign for election, but I didn't care about the money. I was making enough as a consultant to pay our bills; the thing I really wanted was to help the Palestinian people.

When the election was announced for January 25, 2006, the Fatah party asked me to run on its ticket in the October primaries: "We need you with us because we're looking for professional, highly educated, well-trained candidates." At the time, Hamas was not considered to be a contender; it was popular in Gaza, but Fatah still seemed to be in charge. I wanted to run as an independent. Politics in Gaza are tribal, party-based, and entirely dependent on who's paying your salary; I argued that we needed to challenge all that and cultivate a people-based form of politics where ordinary voters truly choose. But Fatah assumed I was running on its ticket, and weighing all the costs and the consequences, I felt I'd better join forces with this party.

I was a neophyte in the ways of electioneering. I thought I knew the score and could hold my own, but soon I was being told what to say, which policy to promote, how to respond to questions. Suddenly, being elected wasn't about who I was and what I stood for; it was about who I was connected to and what I would do for them. As I campaigned all over the northern part of Gaza, the region I hoped to represent, I was seen as a new voice, a man with common sense. But on the day of the primaries, some militants from the Fatah party burst into one of the polling rooms in my district with machine guns. They destroyed the ballot boxes, scared the people nearly to death, and ruined any chance of a fair election. The results in northern Gaza were voided.

An older man I know and respect a lot took me aside and said, "Don't get involved in these dirty games. Run as an independent. I will support you." And I took his advice; no matter the consequences, I was going to run in the upcoming January election as an independent. Upon realizing I was serious about being an independent, Fatah offered me incentives to stay on the ticket (promising to make me deputy prime minister, for example, and to pay for my campaign), but I didn't accept. Instead, I borrowed thirty-five thousand dollars from my brothers and friends to pay my campaign expenses.

As the election date approached, we began to realize the situation was unpredictable. I was campaigning to eradicate poverty, unemployment, and disease, to improve health care and education, and to raise the status of women in Gaza. Hamas was seriously challenging Fatah by running on a platform similar to mine, though its candidates certainly did not campaign on women's issues. Their election slogan was "Repair and Change." What they were vowing to repair was what had been damaged not only by Israeli rocket attacks but also by the Palestinian Authority. Everyone was accusing the PA of mismanagement, corruption, a bad attitude, and of attracting donors who only gave money so they could call the shots. Most Palestinians were upset with the malfeasance of the government. That was what Hamas was vowing to change.

The Hamas campaign was exceptionally well organized. On the day of the vote, its cars picked up constituents, using computers to figure out who was voting and where they lived, and drove them to the polls. In comparison, Fatah was asleep at the switch. I was still confident that I would win in northern Gaza because of the numbers of Gazans who told me they were going to vote for me. Hundreds of people, huge groups, came to support me. On the last day, my children and Nadia came out to campaign for me, urging people to vote for Izzeldin. But on election day itself, 79 percent of the voters cast their ballots for Hamas instead. No independent candidate won anywhere in Gaza. Hamas took 76 of 132 seats in the West Bank and Gaza and became the government.

I guess it says a lot about my nature and determination that I had not even contemplated losing. Still, like other times in my life, good came out of bad. Internal conflict within the new government began almost immediately; I felt lucky that I wasn't part of it. My goal was to make change for the people, to focus on health, education, justice, and women's issues. By midnight on election night, I realized that the loss was actually okay with me. Clearly, this was not my time.

The process was interesting, though. I learned a lot by running in that election. I discovered that when it comes to politics, you can't always count on the people to do what they say they are going to do. Some people show you their full support and then go to the voting booth and cast their ballot for the other party.

Getting out of an election with your reputation intact is tricky enough. But soon after the election, we found out that we had had a crook among us during the campaign, and his actions threatened to drag our family name into the dirt. When we lined up the various computers and pieces of office equipment we had borrowed for the campaign in order to return them, we discovered that many of these items were missing. A man from Jabalia City had come to help us during the campaign; he had stayed at my home and eaten at my table. As we checked off who did what and who was where when, we realized that it was this man who had likely stolen the equipment. I called the police, who arrested him after they found the missing items at his home. Everything was returned to its rightful owners, and the man went to jail. Still, all of it left a bitter taste in my mouth.

Then there were the bigger issues all Gazans soon had to deal with. The peace process had been squandered; the second intifada was a consequence of that failure. Before the election was even called, the Palestinian Authority had told its international partners, the Americans in particular, that it was not ready. However, these so-called partners forced the issue, and Hamas emerged victorious. Since Hamas was deemed a terrorist organization, sanctions were quickly declared against us. The Palestinian people were made to pay—again. But I left that debate to others. With a campaign debt of thirty-five thousand dollars and a family of eight kids to feed, I needed to find a job pronto. We had already sold all of Nadia's gold jewelery as well as the gold we had put away for the children's educations. It was payback time.

The day after the election, I sent my CV to the World Health Organization (WHO). I knew from experience that when Gazans apply to international organizations, even those with an impressive CV, the fact that they come from Gaza may make it much harder for them to get hired. However, my CV must have gone to a wise person who considered my experience without looking at my birthplace, because I heard back almost immediately with the offer of a position as the WHO's health systems and policy adviser to the minister of health in Afghanistan. Taking such a job would mean I would be separated from my family again, but we badly needed the money. There were glitches, of course; after all, this was the Middle East. The WHO required me to visit its offices in Cairo in order to sign the contract, but since Hamas won the election and was deemed a terrorist organization by Israel, as well as by most of Israel's backers, the borders were shut tight. You could not get out. The Israeli authorities said that if I had an invitation to attend a specific event, I would be allowed to cross at Erez and travel to Jordan for a flight to Cairo, but a meeting to sign a contract didn't qualify for an exit permit. So I was stuck in Gaza until the WHO issued me an invitation to a conference in Alexandria. I managed to get permission to go to that and then went on to Cairo to sign the contract. I left from Cairo for Afghanistan in mid-July 2006.

Because Afghanistan was a conflict zone, the work schedule for the job was six weeks on and ten days off. The situation in the country was shocking, even to me. Humanity was intimidated there. The living conditions of most Afghan people reminded me of the descriptions of our villages a hundred years ago. In Gaza we have an unstable political situation and much deprivation, but our systems are far more advanced than the ones in Afghanistan. The airport in Kabul was backward and creaking. It was obvious that the country had been burned by violence. The infrastructure had been destroyed, and most of the systems, from electrical and water to health and social supports, were fragmented and malfunctioning. I thought Gaza was bad; Afghanistan was much worse. Oddly enough, Gazans asked about Afghanistan as though it's the most troubled place on earth, and Afghans asked about Gaza in the same way. The hospitals were old, lacked equipment, and couldn't offer decent patient care. I was actually glad that my job was to make policy and that the position had me spending my time in the office, not on the wards.

I came home every six weeks for ten days, and it was always a celebration when I got back with my bags stuffed with Afghan carpets and traditional Afghan dresses for the children or clothes and jewelry from the Dubai airport. It usually took me three days to get home but only a day and a half back to Kabul (for the usual reasons concerning travel restrictions on Palestinians), and all the travel days came off my ten-day break. I kept up that schedule until June 2007 because the job allowed me to support my family, to repay my campaign debt, and to be in Gaza often enough to keep tabs on what was unfolding. Each visit home was marked by increasingly disturbing incidents.

The situation had become complicated after the election. Mahmoud Abbas was still the leader of the Palestinian Authority even though his Fatah party had been defeated. Although the two sides tried to from a government, the union was on shaky ground from the start and the fighting between the factions was growing worse. It was brother against brother, and violence was spreading both in intensity and in range, until most of the Gaza Strip was involved in one way or another. My country was in danger of imploding.

On June 11, 2007, I was preparing to leave Kabul for the last time and called ahead to say I was coming home via the usual convoluted route through Islamabad, Dubai, and Amman. One of my brothers told me that Hamas had surrounded the house of a Fatah supporter, and later that day I read on the Internet that two brothers had been killed by Hamas at that house. When I got to Dubai and checked the Internet again, I learned that Hamas had declared the northern part of Gaza a military zone and that its soldiers had surrounded the region, taken over the police stations, commandeered the army posts. No one could enter or leave.

I arrived in Jordan on June 13 and hired a taxi to take me to the Erez Crossing. We were at about the halfway point, at Latrun Mountain near Jerusalem, when I called home to ask my brother Nasser to come and pick me up on the Gaza side of the Erez Crossing. Shatha answered the phone, and she told me that Nasser was sick and couldn't come. I didn't believe her. I knew something was very wrong.

As soon as I got through the Erez Crossing, I could feel that Gaza was at a boiling point. Northern Gaza had been turned into an armed camp totally controlled by Hamas. The Palestinian National Guards who normally check people at the border were standing at the side of the road, too frightened to move. The streets were empty. It was as though war had been declared.

When I got home, my brother Atta explained how close this war had come to our home. Our nephew Mohammed, Nasser's son, had been shot in the knees and ankles; his father had not been too sick to come to the border for me—he was too distraught. Mohammed was an officer with the National Guard of the Palestinian Authority, and he'd been shot by Hamas gunmen in an act of revenge, presumably for taking the side of Fatah. There were many young men between the ages of twenty-two and twenty-four in northern Gaza who were wounded and bleeding. Nasser hoped I could help, but I couldn't even get to most of them at first. The Palestinian Authority's security bases had been taken over by Hamas, and for one awful week, from June 13 to June 20, there was full-out civil war. By the time it was over, Hamas had routed the Fatah forces and taken control of the Gaza Strip.

We stayed inside for the duration—no one dared to go out on the street. When we needed food, we plotted a course to the market, ventured out, then scurried home again. There was gunfire all around, shooting on every street. With civil war you never know who the enemy really is. I'd spent the last year in Afghanistan seeing the same confusion of tribal, political, and ideological warfare. Here in my own Gaza, I wasn't sure who was fighting against whom. When the street-to-street fighting lessened, I arranged for some of the severely wounded, including my nephew Mohammed, to be transferred to Soroka hospital. Mohammed was in the hospital for two months. The doctors saved his legs, but he still walks with a severe limp.

At the time he was wounded, Mohammed was a twenty-four-year-old university student working with the Palestinian National Guard in order to support his family. He was forced to take this position when my brother Nasser lost his job in Israel after the closing of the Gaza-Israeli border made it impossible for him to get to work. Mohammed was on duty when Hamas militants attacked their base in the northern part of the Gaza Strip, about 550 yards from my home. Many of his commanders were killed, and many others, including a paramedic, were severely injured. Mohammed and some of his co-workers fled the base and hid in a store, but Hamas ended up searching the store and found them. They were tied up, blindfolded, beaten, and tortured. They were then thrown into a Hamas vehicle and told to get out near Al Awda hospital. They were ordered to line up facing a wall. There, they awaited their fate, which was to be shot. But Palestinians from the surrounding area were watching what was happening and took action, pushing the young men down to prevent Hamas from shooting them in the heads. As a result, the bullets pierced their lower limbs, their ankles and knees. They were left there to bleed to death. They needed to be taken to the better-equipped Al Quds hospital in Gaza City to be stabilized, since they were in shock due to severe bleeding. Mohammed was transfused with eight BT units of blood.

I arrived at the hospital to find it packed with young men with severe injuries to their lower limbs. Mohammed was in serious condition. I found out that he had been operated on the night before, but when I asked for the medical report, there was nothing written in it. I had to find out from my brother Nasser that he had fractures and vascular injuries. Due to the large number of patients with severe injuries, none of the medical staff could answer any of my questions. I had never seen so many young men screaming in pain and agony, asking for help, but with no response since there were only one or two nurses on duty in the entire department. Ambulances were arriving nonstop, bringing still more injured people. I thought of transferring Mohammed to an Israeli hospital, but what about the others? They were all equal and facing the same challenges.

After a couple of days, Mohammed's condition deteriorated even further; he suffered from fever, anemia, and severe pain. With the shortage of medications, medicine needed to be bought from outside the hospital. The attending physician was the one who decided that my nephew's medical condition was among the most dire, so he had him transferred to an Israeli hospital. At that point, I spoke to my colleagues at Soroka hospital in Israel and was assured that they would treat him. However, due to the border closing between Gaza and Israel, it would still be two more days before the transfer could take place. Security still would not allow it, so I started to call all my friends and use all my connections, and after extensive efforts he was finally transferred. He spent one month in Soroka hospital and had three surgeries that saved his legs. He was returned to Gaza with crutches and in a wheelchair and had two further months of physiotherapy. I found out later that many of his friends who had been left to be treated in Gaza ended up with amputations of their limbs.

I was heartbroken with the turn of events in Gaza. How could we heal this new wound and cope with the resulting scar? The

Israelis were the enemy, but now we'd become enemies inside our own house too.

At that point, any progress we'd made started going into reverse. The Israelis responded to the conflict by creating even more draconian restrictions on access to and goods for Gaza. As a result, the medical staff in Gaza was faced with increasing challenges, including a lack of security, a shortage of medications, insufficient resources to be able to help the many patients with complex injuries, and inadequate training leading to a shortage of skills and experience. The suffering inside the Strip increased, and as it did, so did the rocket attacks on Israeli towns near the Gaza border.

The last decade has been a particularly disappointing period in this grinding conflict that keeps us apart. Our leaders bicker like children, breaking promises, behaving like bullies, keeping the kettle of trouble boiling. The people I talk to—patients, doctors, neighbors in Gaza, friends in Israel—are not like our leaders. They worry about my family as I worry about their families. We all lament the lost decades, the uncertain future. However, as incredible as it may sound to someone watching us from afar, we believe in each other and in our ability to share this Holy Land. It is quite astonishing to realize how similar our two peoples are, in the way we raise our children, in the importance of family and extended family, and in the animated style with which we like to tell stories. We're argumentative, expressive, emotional people. We share the Semitic religions and languages. We have many more similarities than differences, and yet for sixty years we haven't been able to bridge the divide between us.

How is it that we can look at one life and say it is more valuable than another one? Look at the infants in the delivery rooms: they are innocent children who have the right to grow up to be educated adults with opportunities in life. Then we fill them with stories that promote hatred and fear. Every human life is invaluable, and so easy to destroy with bullets and bombs or with the accusations and revisionist history that promote hatred. Hatred eats at your soul and takes opportunities away from you. It's like consuming poison.

Ever since my time at Harvard, I've received invitations to come back to the United States to speak about Israeli-Palestinian relations. Sometimes at those events I receive comments from people who really don't know what it is to live with so much conflict. To be honest, though, some of the people aren't really interested in asking a question; they just want to use the opportunity to give their own speeches. On plenty of occasions I have been interrupted, shouted down, and accused of not seeing the other side. Most people in the audience wait until the shouting dies down in order to hear what I came to talk about. I tell them—both the sympathetic and the hostile—how we need to go about solving the problems we share with Israel. For example, when people tell me that after many years of occupying Gaza the Israeli soldiers left and we should be grateful for that, I try to explain to them that the way the departure happened created more problems than it solved. Any such major move needs to be coordinated with your partner. The lack of discussion created chaos, and the Palestinians were blamed.

At one speaking engagement, all these things happened at once: the interruptions, the shouting, and the accusing. But once I got past the unpleasantness, I found that the questions were thoughtful and well intended. For example, one person asked, "What can we do here, as Israelis in the United States, to encourage dialogue?" Another said, "It's great that you're here talking to us, but are you also making this same plea for peace on the other side, in your own community?" My reply was that yes, of course, I make that same plea, and that this sort of conversation is exactly what we need to be having. If we don't air our grievances, we'll never get past them.

Still, one man pointedly asked, "You speak of dialogue between the two nations, but whom do we have to talk to—Hamas? You say we need to respect one another, but your elected leaders are not even willing to recognize the existence of the state of Israel. What kind of respect is that?" All I could do was try to explain that there is a way out of this turmoil; that we need to move forward and stop being mired in what went before. It sounds simplistic, but it's the only way to get out of the mud our feet are stuck in. The occupation and oppression of the people in Gaza is like a cancer, a disease that needs to be treated. It's all about the will to solve the problem rather than the determination to keep the anger front and center. Arguing over who did what and who suffered more is not getting us anywhere. We have to move on; we have to build trust and mutual respect between the peoples. You can't respect someone you don't know. So let's get to know one another by listening and opening our eyes to the other side. We need to encourage *kavod* (respect) and *shivyon* (equality).

Also, we need to focus on realistic goals. Grand plans for peace have failed us. We need to look at what's possible right now: working toward both sides having more equal conditions, with equal rights and mutual respect.

Some say I'm wearing rose-colored glasses, that I refuse to see the hopelessness of the situation. Maybe they're right. I never see anything as hopeless—not when I'm delivering a baby that's in distress, not when I'm staunching the blood flow from a woman who is hemorrhaging, and not when I'm treating a dozen other ills that have been diagnosed as untreatable. So why would I see the quarrel between two people as hopeless? I care about people. I'm no different from anyone else. We are created like that: to be social, to live with other people. Segregation is unnatural.

But I'm getting ahead of my story.

By the summer of 2007, I was looking for a job again. I had decided not to renew my contract with the WHO in Afghanistan because it had meant too much time away from my family and it was way too tense in Gaza. I concentrated on getting contract work, lecturing at Ben-Gurion University in the Columbia International Medical Program, treating patients in Gaza, and picking up European Union consultancy jobs here and there.

The previous December I had been invited to the Third National Conference on Health Policy in Jerusalem. Getting there had been the usual trial, but chasing after the permits and exercising patience turned out to be worth the trouble: at that conference I met Mordechai Shani, the director and founder of the Gertner Institute. Founded in 1991, the institute serves as a national research setting for the study of epidemiology and health policy. It does extensive research on major chronic diseases and assists in the formulation of national health policy. I was fascinated by this sort of work. As a physician, I had been wondering for many years how to deal with the many Palestinian families afflicted by such prevalent genetic disorders as thalassemia, an inherited recessive blood disease affecting the hemoglobin, and hermaphroditism, where a child is born with both male and female reproductive organs. Then there are congenital disorders like phocomelia, a malformation in which babies are born with limbs that look like flippers on a seal, and anophthalmia, the congenital absence of one or both eyes.

The patients weren't getting the help they needed, nor were the families, and no one was doing research in this area. I wondered if this Gertner Institute could be the place that would conduct studies on these medical anomalies. But there were more immediate research questions to be answered, about the Palestinian patients who were currently coming to Israeli hospitals for treatment, for instance. Who are they? What are the numbers, ages, and sexes of these patients? What ailments and diseases bring them into the hospital? How big a problem is this? Research proposals were pouring into my mind even as Mordechai Shani was describing his institute. I knew right away that I wanted to work there, and I asked if I could have a meeting with him. Mordechai is a man of action and few words, and he makes decisions the same way. After I explained my interests and my background to him, he said, "Start your research immediately," which I did. Before the year 2007 ended, I was on staff at the Gertner Institute at the Sheba hospital in Tel Aviv.

The contract work I had already been doing allowed me to travel all over the Gaza Strip and gave me an opportunity to crunch the numbers that I felt told the story of present-day Gaza as well as explain the sources of some of its medical problems: the unemployment, the deprivation due to the blockade, the deteriorating health, social, and economic structures. It's never been easy in Gaza, but it's been a lot worse in the last few years. Almost everything can be measured in terms of loss. Agriculture, for example, is down to half of its usual harvest, and productivity in industry has dropped an astonishing 90 percent. There are almost no construction materials coming into the Gaza Strip, and certain medicines are banned. The Israelis have even calculated the number of calories a person needs to survive and allow only bare essentials to cross the border into the Strip. Fruits such as apricots, plums, grapes, and avocados, even dairy products, are suddenly declared nonessential and forbidden to us. What's going on here? Whose goals are these?

The stiffening embargo, the incursions, attacks, and arrests are playing on the psyches of the people. What's worse is that we Gazans don't see the outside world caring much about our plight. That adds to the angst. Our politicians bicker about who said what and who will recognize whom and then change their minds when a new slate of officials is elected. All this while babies die from malnutrition, mothers bleed to death in childbirth, and an old lady with cancer is held up at the Erez Crossing because someone is trying to teach someone else a lesson.

The International Committee of the Red Cross (ICRC) has criticized the current embargo. A November 2007 report titled *Dignity Denied in the Occupied Palestinian Territories* said:

> Palestinians face hardship in their daily lives; they are prevented from doing what makes up the daily fabric of most people's existence. They face a deep human crisis, where millions of people are denied their human dignity. Not once in a while, but every day, and the people of Gaza are trapped and sealed off. The humanitarian cost is enormous, people can barely survive, families unable to get enough food increased by 14 percent, and Palestinians are being trampled underfoot day after day. In Gaza under siege, Palestinians continue to pay for conflict and economic containment with their health and livelihoods.

We've learned to do without, manage with less, and cope with deprivation over and over and over again—for sixty years now.

If anyone thinks this does not have an effect on the physical and mental state of the people, that person needs to come to Gaza to check for himself. The situation is simply not tenable, and I'm not the only one to describe it this way. The ICRC confirms that "every day, 69 million liters of partially treated or completely untreated sewage—the equivalent of 28 Olympic-size swimming pools—are pumped directly into the Mediterranean because they cannot be treated." When I was a boy, we didn't have running water in the house. Now, fifty years later, we have access to running water, but only on certain days. Why? Because, like everything else in Gaza, the water supply system is damaged and the materials needed to repair it sit on an embargo list.

Everyone in Gaza scrounges for old parts and broken concrete to patch their lives together. The water and sanitation services are on the verge of collapse. One can only imagine the size of the public health catastrophe that threatens us. This is what I mean when I tell people that Gaza could implode. Imagine if we were faced with waterborne illnesses. Imagine the chaos, the unnecessary deaths. Imagine the laying of blame: people would say, if spare parts and water pipes hadn't been stopped at the border, no one would have died.

I have been trying to alert the authorities to the consequences of a broken health care system for more than a decade. Now the Red Cross is sounding the same clarion call:

Gaza's health-care system cannot provide the treatment that many patients suffering from serious illness require. Tragically, a number of them are not allowed to leave the Strip in time to seek health care elsewhere. Health issues in Gaza are often politicized and patients find themselves caught up in a bureaucratic maze. The procedures for requesting permission to leave the territory are complicated and involve both the Palestinian and Israeli authorities. Seriously ill patients sometimes have to wait for months before the relevant authorities allow them to leave the Gaza Strip. Even when patients do obtain the necessary permits to leave, the transfer through Erez Crossing into Israel can be arduous. Patients on life-support machines have to be removed from ambulances and placed on stretchers then carried 60–80 meters [approximately 65–90 yards] through the crossing to ambulances waiting on the other side. Patients who can walk unassisted may face extensive questioning before they are allowed through the crossing for medical treatment—or, as sometimes happens, before they are refused entry into Israel and turned back.

Some of the health issues have been addressed, some even solved. But every time there's a change of government on either side, the rules for transfer and treatment also change. It's a life-threatening situation that creates rage among those who have to endure it. Here are the facts the Red Cross reports:

[The Gazans] depend on a timely and reliable supply of medicines from the Palestinian Authority's Ministry of Health in the West Bank, but the supply chain often breaks down. Co-operation between the health authorities in the West Bank and Gaza is difficult. Complex and lengthy Israeli import procedures also hamper the reliable supply of even the most basic items such as painkillers and X-ray film developers. As a result, some patients, including people suffering from cancer or kidney failure, do not always get the essential drugs they need.

For example, the ventilators for newborns at Al-Shifa hospital are out of order. It's not possible to get spare parts to fix them. How do you explain to a mother and father that their baby will die because the truck with the parts for the ventilator is being held at the border?

Gaza has been the center of war so many times, it's not surprising that the number of Gazans who have lost limbs is high. Dozens of amputees wait for treatment. Why? Does importing artificial limbs pose a security risk? Or is this about punishment? How do you explain this to a five-year-old who lost a limb when his house fell on him after it was shelled by the Israeli army, or to an angry young man who can't get off the floor to learn to walk again?

That the Gaza hospitals are run-down and can't be repaired because of an embargo is preposterous. This is a medical issue; it's not about recruiting soldiers and making rockets. Here are the facts as reported by the ICRC:

Much of the equipment is unreliable and in need of repair. Complicated procedures for obtaining approval to import spare parts make it difficult and time-consuming to bring in and maintain hospital equipment, such as CT scanners, and spare parts—even for hospital washing machines. Daily power cuts and power fluctuations continue to damage medical equipment. Most hospitals have to rely on backup generators for several hours a day, but it is never certain that enough fuel will be available to run them.

Seventy percent of Gazans are officially below the poverty line, with incomes of less than US$250 per month for a family of seven to nine. Forty percent are classified as extremely poor, with incomes of US$120 per month or less. Because of industry shutdowns, seventy thousand jobs have disappeared.

Unemployment stands at 44 percent. Much of the time, we rely on goods coming through the tunnels that have been dug underground into Egypt, but the tunnels can't begin to meet the needs of 1.5 million people. What's more, they're regularly bombed by the Israeli air force.

Even farming, which has always been part of the lifestyle and economy of Gaza, is in danger because of the embargo. Gaza used to export tons of fruits and vegetables and thousands of workers to Israel. Not anymore—there's no place for farmers to sell their produce. Drive around Gaza and you can see the evidence. Drainage ditches are destroyed, and so are greenhouses and water wells. Irrigation systems have been wrecked by military operations, and trees have been uprooted. The ICRC examined the issue and found that many farmers "are effectively denied access to parts of their land because of the Israeli-imposed 'no-go' zone on the Gaza side of the border fence with Israel."

At least 30 percent of the arable land in Gaza lies within this buffer zone, which can extend up to one kilometer [.62 mile] from the fence. A farmer never knows for sure if it is safe to work his land or to harvest within the zone. Farmers risk being shot at when tending to their land and incursions by the army often leave fields and parts of the harvest destroyed. Getting agricultural production up and running again is difficult not only because of the destruction that has occurred, but also because Israel does not allow the importation of suitable fertilizers and because many types of seedlings are difficult or even impossible to find in Gaza.

Fishing faces the same impossible restrictions: Gaza's boats are not allowed past the three-nautical-mile limit, which effectively cuts our fishery off from the bigger species and the sardines that made up 70 percent of the catch before the 2007 embargo was enforced. Israeli gunboats guard the perimeter, aiming their guns by day and night along the shore and at the small boats of hapless fishermen. In other words, Gazans are trapped. Even students I know who have received scholarships to study in the United States have been denied exit visas from Gaza. In 2008 a boy with a Fulbright scholarship had to turn this huge opportunity down because he couldn't get the permit he needed.

The ICRC has appealed for the lifting of restrictions on the movement of people and goods as the first and most urgent measure to end Gaza's isolation and allow its people to rebuild their lives. The report says:

A lasting solution requires fundamental changes in Israeli policy, such as allowing imports and exports to and from Gaza, increasing the flow of goods and people up to the level of May 2007, allowing farmers to access their land in the de-facto buffer zone and restoring fishermen's access to deeper waters. Humanitarian action can be no substitute for the credible political steps that are needed to bring about these changes. Only an honest and courageous political process involving all States, political authorities and organized armed groups concerned can address the plight of Gaza and restore a dignified life to its people. The alternative is a further descent into misery with every passing day.

This report, from an internationally recognized organization that has a reputation for not taking sides, is of great value to both Gazans and Israelis. But I have to admit that, coupled with the information I have gathered myself in the villages and camps and cities of the Gaza Strip, the ICRC report struck a discouraging blow to the psyche of a man who has believed with all his heart that the situation can and must improve.

I find myself holding on tightly to the knowledge that Israeli doctors feel as I do: the humanitarian work we undertake as physicians is a bridge across the divide; it can help untangle the distrust and promote a relationship that can lead us out of this quagmire. The director general of the Sheba Medical Center in Tel Aviv is Dr. Zeev Rotstein. He has a vision for this region that can become a reality through health care. I'll let him explain his own views about how medical teams can reach across the divide:

I'm a cardiologist. Part of my job before the [first] intifada was the diagnosis and treatment of congenital heart disease among children, specifically in Gaza and the West Bank. My heart is with those children who can't get the treatment they need. I used to go there once a week to evaluate them and refer them for treatment. Before the intifada the population there was much better off from a health point of view. They had full access to medical services and good follow-up in Israel free of charge, plus Gaza doctors were being trained here in Israel. But since the last intifada started—and I'm trying to avoid politics here—to my eyes, the children are the ones who are paying the full price. The training of physicians stopped. Access to medical services isn't as smooth as it was. It's really affected by the politics in the area. I always keep that in mind when collaborating with our colleagues from Gaza. We're trying to promote health and alleviate misery and disease. From the very beginning, I declared an open door for those children who are diagnosed in two specific fields. One is cancer—we can cure more than half of the cancers and 88 percent of blood cancers. The second set of diseases we can help tremendously is congenital heart disease. We can take these blue children and transform them into pink children. Without this, they die in misery, suffering complications of congenital heart disease. We can do this, we really can do it. It's just a matter of being stubborn.

Izzeldin has a very good record of treating these cases. His mission was defined as one that would evaluate and define epidemiologically the effect a bilateral relationship had on those children. He was fighting for better medical services, better follow-up and productivity in closing the circle. He was improving the treatment by closing the loop. For example, a child can get treatment here in Israel but goes home and has no support and a lack of continuation of care. I saw Izzeldin as a kind of coordinator. By his research activity he improved results for those kids. He worked here and there collecting data. Unfortunately, the only data available to him on this side was from Tel Hashomer [Sheba hospital]. Not everyone wanted to collaborate. They made it difficult to collect medical material from them. Here our files are computerized and we're open to this kind of activity and sympathize with it.

Izzeldin says health care can be an important bridge between two peoples. I agree with him. It works because saving a life and not giving up and doing that over and over again gives the other side the opportunity to see the face of Israelis, not through rifles, but through health care. People who were born and raised there come here for treatment. They don't know us. They don't know how sensitive we are about life. They don't know the real Israeli. Palestinians are incited from birth. They tell us that they never imagined we were human, that they thought we were monsters, conquerors, people who wanted to see them dead. Then they're treated by us and are surprised that those things are not true.

The majority of Israelis want to live side by side. I'm sure it's that way with Palestinians as well. But we're led by extremists on both sides. It's so easy to incite the people with the misery they are in.

The Israeli patients I treat don't care that I'm a Palestinian doctor; they care about having someone to help them with their medical problem. The Gazans don't care that I work in Israel; they care about finding security in their lives and getting treatment for their children. And yet I continue to meet people who are shocked that a Palestinian doctor treats Jewish patients. There is a presumption that we hate each other, that each side wants the other side dead. I'm sure those sentiments exist among some of the people, but in my experience it's not nearly the number of people the rhetoric suggests.

The important thing about bridging the divide is admitting the truth, the facts around people's lives today. For example, "the right of return"—the topic everyone knows about but no one wants to discuss. Hundreds of thousands of Palestinians were deported when Israel became a state. Everyone knows this fact. The BBC program *Panorama* aired a documentary about the people who live close to my ancestral village today. You can hear individuals in the film saying, "This is Abuelaish land." It's important for the Israelis to admit their moral and political responsibility and start building trust, which is the only way to arrive at an acceptable solution in which both sides can live in partnership and collaboration. We cannot continue to ignore the issue; there have to be solutions. It's all about building ties, knowing each other, finding the way together. Of course it can be done. It's all a matter of will. But every time we seem to be approaching a level of trust that could bring us together, there's a new outbreak of violence and hopes are dashed again.

I am not alone in my belief in bridging the divide. There are peace camps and summer schools and "surfers for peace" and hip-hop rappers beating out peace messages. There are endless school projects and Web sites devoted to peace, and there's even a peace phone line. There are examples of coexistence throughout Gaza and the West Bank and Israel. You can find midwives on both sides of the line promoting peaceful coexistence. Look at the Web site of the Circle of Health International: Coexistence in the Middle East. The Palestinian project coordinator, Aisha Saifi, says, "I have been volunteering and working with COHI for the past three years and the experience has completely changed me. As a Palestinian woman, a mother, and a midwife, not only has this organization allowed me to help the women and children of my country, but it has also enabled me to deliver my message of peace and harmony." The Israeli coordinator, Gomer Ben Moshe, says, "Belonging to a group of midwives who are willing to volunteer, being part of a mutual dialogue with Palestinian midwives, fills me with energy and motivation. I believe women should take part in brokering peace and midwifery is an international language that can be spoken by all women in the world."

There are even basketball leagues for Arab-Israeli and Jewish teenagers who believe in promoting coexistence and tolerance, and an industrial project on the northern border between Israel and the West Bank whose raison d'être is coexistence. There are conferences all over the world devoted to finding a way to bring Palestinians and Israelis together. And yet harmony eludes us.

One of the ways to alter the status quo is to look to the women and girls. It's easy to find a thousand men in favor of war; it's difficult to find five women who are inclined that way. It's clearly time to empower Palestinian women and girls, to give them respect and independence and let them take the lead. Too many girls cannot get an education because of financial and cultural considerations. Too many families with limited resources give chances only to their sons even though their daughters are also serious and committed. I can understand their reasoning: a son is expected to support his parents in their old age, while a daughter usually moves away after marriage to live with her husband's family. If a father doesn't have enough money to educate all his children, he might decide it's better to educate his sons, believing that his daughters will be taken care of by the families into which they marry. But the first phrase in the Quran speaks of the importance of education:

1. Read! in the name of thy Lord and Cherisher, Who created-
2. Created man, out of a mere clot of congealed blood: 3. Read! And thy Lord is Most Bountiful, 4. He Who taught the use of the pen.

And it doesn't differentiate between educating men and women. We have a saying that goes like this: The mother is the school. If you prepare this school with the right equipment, the students will be smarter and more successful and so will the nation. Consider the studies done by the World Bank and the North-South Institute that have found that if you pay attention to the health and education of the women in a community, the economy of the village will turn around. The World Bank has done these studies every five years since 1985; there is evidence beyond any doubt that investing in women and girls is the way out of poverty and conflict.

I grew up watching the way women in Gaza raised their children. I saw the decision making and the perseverance, but I understood that the women weren't being given the opportunity to bring their own expertise to the table. Women and girls are not able to rise to their potential in Gaza, and as a result they cannot participate to their fullest.

A healthy society needs wise and educated women. An educated and healthy woman will raise an educated and healthy family. We need to link education with health care, and the most effective way to do that is to make sure that education and health care are available to women. It's an investment that can shift not only the thinking but the power in the Middle East. Removing the barriers that confront our women and girls could very well lead us to peaceful coexistence.

These were the issues that were on my mind when I started my job at the Gertner Institute, and they stayed with me as my research work continued throughout the winter and spring of 2008. I enjoyed my work, but being away from home from Sunday to Thursday took its toll. Every Monday morning I would begin counting the days until I could go home to be with my family. I tried to make the three-day weekend feel like a five-day week. Nadia had done most of the parenting by herself over the years, but the kids were older now, and I worried about them in a way I never had before. Nadia needed me by her side, and I wanted to be there.

One weekend night, I overheard Mayar saying to her sister, "The worst times are when Father is traveling." That hit me hard. What was I doing, being away from them so much? Who knew how long I would live? My work was important, yes, but my family was everything to me.

Conditions in Gaza continued to deteriorate, and I continued to have to pass through excruciating, time-consuming security back and forth at the Erez Crossing, or the Rafah Crossing between Gaza and Egypt. Yes, at least I was allowed to cross, but the frustration and the humiliation were a constant burden. I was so happy to hear Mayar say she thought their worst times were when I was away, because I sometimes believed the worst times were when I brought my anger and humiliation home. For any human being, freedom is essential, crucial, to our dignity and our ability to be fully human.

Anger and violence in Gaza and among Gazans is completely predictable. In a situation like ours, the absence of violence and anger would be abnormal. All of us feel angry at least occasionally. Most of the time when I get angry, I get over it quickly, but to my regret, only after I have upset others. Controlling one's anger is the right way to cope, but this is easier said than done. Whenever I lash out, I almost immediately am full of regret. Why didn't I control myself? Why did I allow myself to hurt my loved ones? Why did I do this to my wife and children?

All I can say is that frustrations build up. I remember one day in particular: When I arrive home, I am physically exhausted from the crossing. My children need me, yet it feels like I am helpless to go to them; there are so many hurdles in the way. I've watched someone else be humiliated by the guards. I've seen a patient tired and weak from cancer arbitrarily barred from crossing for treatment he should have received two weeks ago. I can do nothing. I have no control over the situation.

Then I walk in the door, and my beloved wife, Nadia, greets me with all the problems of the day, problems I care deeply about: Mohammed didn't do his homework. (He must do his homework. He must study. Education is the only possible avenue out of a life of hopelessness.) Abdullah didn't listen to his mother and was playing in the street with his cousins again. (Abdullah must not play in the street. Why doesn't he listen? Why can't Nadia control him? Why isn't there a park where children can play safely? Recently, he was hit by a car and had to be taken to the hospital. He could have been killed. Why are the drivers so reckless with all the children playing in the only place available to them? The driver had no insurance. I had to cover the hospital bills myself.) Dalal said she was going to visit her aunt Yousra for a few hours, but she stayed overnight, returning the next day nonchalantly. (How can she stay overnight without asking or even informing us? This is unacceptable. She is part of this family. We are linked together, and we must know where she is. Something could have happened to her.)

I listen restlessly. I go to my desk to respond to some e-mails and answer phone messages. There is one message written down, which is apparently important: "Mohammed wants you to call him back." I ask, "Mohammed who?" But no one knows. In Palestine, the name Mohammed is like John is in North America; there are a thousand Mohammeds. What can I do with this information? It's useless. I go to make a note about something I need to do and discover that the notepad by my desk is missing (yet again). No one takes responsibility. I go to the refrigerator to check out what we need so I can make a shopping list, and discover rotten food. It's the last straw: I explode, throwing the rotten food on the floor. I shout at my wife, "I didn't inherit this money, nor did I steal it—I sweat for it. You open the refrigerator at least ten times a day, yet you don't have the time to throw out the rotten food. How many times does this have to happen? Why can't you be more careful?"

The children cower, and Nadia goes to her brother's house because she's so upset by my yelling. She also knows it's better to leave me alone to calm down. I go off by myself to try to do just that.

I realize I lose my temper because home is safe. I can't explode in front of the officials. It would be utterly disastrous. I would lose everything. I would be detained further. I wouldn't be able to leave Gaza for work, for study, or for medical reasons. If I were trying to get back into Palestine, I wouldn't be able to come home.

The drums of discontent on both sides were beating like early warning signals in the summer of 2008. I could see no hope for change in the short term. I decided I owed it to my children and to Nadia to find a job in a place where we could be together, where there wouldn't be such blatant restrictions on us as the border demanded, where the kids could be safe to go to school, to play on the street, and to be themselves. I wanted to take them away from the tension that infects everyone like a virus in the Middle East. Not forever—this is still my homeland. But for a while—just to give the family a chance to grow up, to be together. So in August 2008, when I received a notice from an international organization about health policy jobs in Kenya and Uganda and another one through the European Union in Brussels, I decided to book a ticket and find out if there was something out there in the wide world for me and my loved ones.

FIVE

Loss

If life were normal in Gaza, my flight out of the region on August 16, 2008, would have been simple: drive to the checkpoint, exit Gaza, enter Israel, continue by car to the Ben-Gurion International Airport in Tel Aviv, and fly to any place in the world. However, life is not normal, and that airport is off-limits to Palestinians. The only way to travel abroad is by way of Jordan; the routes through Israel and Egypt, our closest neighbors, are not open to us unless we have a very special permit, which is almost impossible to obtain. I didn't know it at the time, but that awkward, problem-filled journey I took out of Gaza in the summer of 2008—not much different from the experience of any Palestinian who needs to travel—was the beginning of the end in more ways than I could possibly have imagined.

A project being operated by Population Services International (PSI) in Kenya and Uganda was looking to hire a consultant in reproductive health. If I could get the position, maybe this was finally the time to move my family out of Gaza to a place where we wouldn't be oppressed and where we would have access to the rest of the world. I had spent my adult life determined to improve health and education in the Gaza Strip and to be one of the architects of coexistence with Israel. But I also worried about my children: if I had the opportunity to move them someplace safe, someplace where it was easier for them to fulfill their potential, shouldn't I listen to my heart?

As a first step, I agreed to fly to Nairobi to participate in a two-week training course for HIV/AIDS and reproductive health programs. The plan was that I'd then fly on to Kampala, Uganda, to meet the staff with whom I would be working if I chose to take the position and then to Brussels for another potential employment opportunity with the European Union.

I began my quest early to get the paperwork I needed for the trip. Two weeks before my planned departure date, I booked my ticket to fly from Amman, Jordan, to Nairobi via Cairo. Then I made the arrangements for the exit permits I would need: one from Gaza to go through the Erez Crossing, the other to exit Israel via the Allenby Bridge, which joins the east and west banks of the Jordan River. The bridge, built in 1918 by the British general Edmund Allenby, is the designated exit from Israel for Palestinians going to Jordan.

But this is the Middle East, and in particular the Palestinian territory; here the best-laid plans go awry, and that's what happened to mine. I did my usual stint at the Sheba hospital in Tel Aviv but headed home a day earlier than usual, on August 13, to spend extra time with my wife and children before I left. At the Erez Crossing, I was informed that the border would be closed on Saturday, August 16, and that I wouldn't be able to get out that day to make my flight. The official I spoke with suggested I leave Friday and stay in the West Bank, as the restrictions there are less severe than the ones at the Gaza crossings, but I didn't want to lose time with my family. So I asked to see the officer in charge, who said, "Don't worry. I will fix it. You will cross on Saturday."

On Thursday afternoon, though, I received a call from the security office in Tel Aviv saying I could not travel—at all! I only had forty-eight hours before I was to catch a plane in Amman to get to Nairobi, and I was being told I could not leave Gaza. I asked what on earth was going on, and he said, "For security reasons you cannot travel." I work in Israel, for heaven's sake. How can this be? It must be a mistake.

After I hung up, I called my friend Shlomi Eldar, a well-known Israeli television journalist who also writes for various Israeli publications. We had met at the Erez Crossing a couple of years earlier when he was coming into Gaza with a cameraman to shoot a story. I had read a book he'd just published on Gaza, and started a conversation with him about whether he had understood the politics correctly. It was the beginning of many useful exchanges of information between Shlomi and me. When he heard my story on the phone that day, he said he was as perplexed as I was. "If you can't travel, then no Palestinian can travel. What is going on? My only weapon is my pen. I'm going to write about this." He called the officer at the Erez Crossing to interview him, while I called another Israeli friend, who said he would check into it and call me back. A few minutes later the phone rang, and it was my friend, who said, "They're serious. They don't want you to travel. You need to wait another week." Why now? What about my plane ticket, my appointments, my job interview, and my training? What was I supposed to do about that? And how could I allow these security people to put a black mark against my name? Come to think of it, how could they allow me to continue to work in Israel if I was a security threat? None of it made sense.

At seven o'clock that night, my phone rang. It was an employee from the office of the coordinator of security for the state of Israel, who asked me what was going on. When I explained the situation to him, he replied, "Every problem can be solved. You can travel on Saturday." So I presumed the mix-up had been sorted out.

There was no one but the guards at the crossing on Saturday. It felt eerie to walk alone through the long corridors, sidestep the rolls of barbed wire, and find my way through the maze of X-ray machines, locked doorways, and interrogators. When I got to the other side and handed my papers to the Israeli security officer, guess what she said? "You can't travel."

"Why not?" I asked.

"For security reasons," she replied. That's bureaucrat-speak for "We have no reason. We've just decided to pick on you." But I wasn't exactly holding any free-pass cards here; she had all the power. I had to bite my tongue. One wrong word or a misplaced gesture could derail my entire trip. So I politely asked her to check with her boss about my so-called security status. It took an hour for her to process that request. When she was done, she told me that I was allowed to proceed to the taxi that would take me to the Allenby Bridge.

So, with a handful of papers, a pocketful of coins to pay the various taxi and bus drivers, and my heart full of hope, I headed for the bridge. You would assume that, having passed scrutiny at Erez, all I'd have to do was show my papers to the Israeli officials at the bridge and cross. You'd be wrong. Because of the extraordinary suspicion between our two sides, the procedure at Allenby resembles a spy movie. I got out of the taxi that brought me there, paying what the driver demanded, and deposited my luggage on a trolley being guarded by an official who looked at me as though I were personally responsible for every wound the two peoples have dealt each other over the past sixty years. Then I boarded a bus to the Palestinian passport section, where my papers were thoroughly inspected. After they were approved, I returned to the bus, which drove me about two thirds of a mile to the luggage depository, where I picked out my screened bags from the heap on the ground. Then I reboarded the bus for the short drive to the Jordanian side.

There I began again, this time with Jordanian officials. I presented my papers, including the visa for Jordan that I'd applied for weeks earlier, and was directed to a special window designated for Gazans. I waited there for what felt like an eternity, especially in light of the flight I needed to catch in Amman. A Palestinian designation on your papers is enough to warrant a very long wait wherever you are in this part of the world. At last my luggage was checked again, and I was cleared to go. I had left at seven thirty A.M. for a journey that in a normal world would involve merely a one-hour drive to the airport in Amman. I barely made it in time to catch the six P.M. flight, but I considered the day a success because I was actually able to board my plane.

The training course in Nairobi lasted two weeks. My wife's niece was married on August 26, and I was sorry I couldn't be there. I knew that everyone had been looking forward to the celebration, and during a business trip to Yemen a few months earlier, I had purchased beautiful silk dresses for my daughters and my wife to wear. I knew they would want to share the family gossip about the wedding and maybe boast a little about how they'd looked in their dresses, so I called home the next day. During our telephone conversation, Nadia told me she was tired and not feeling very well. I teased her about having too good a time at the wedding, dancing late into the night, and she laughed and told me not to be concerned.

When my training was completed, I carried on as planned to Kampala to meet with the Population Service International staff. After a few days there (and a quick shopping trip to buy colorful scarves for my wife and daughters), I left for Egypt on

September 1. Since it was the first day of Ramadan, I called home to give my family my blessings for this new holy month. Mayar answered the phone, and I could tell something was amiss by the sound of her voice. I spoke to Bessan as well, and grew certain they were keeping something from me. Usually everyone in the house would rush to the phone to speak to me when I called from wherever I was, but this time it was only Mayar and Bessan who wanted to talk. But then again, I'd called at midnight and perhaps they were tired, or had just woken up for the first prayers of the day. I told Mayar to give everyone my love, but as I hung up, prickling concerns played on my mind as if to reinforce the notion that it was time to move my family to a place where we could all prosper together.

It turned out that what Mayar and Bessan were not telling me was that the fatigue their mother had complained about only a few days before had increased to a debilitating level, and she had been taken to Al-Shifa hospital in Gaza. She had instructed the children to keep the news from me so that I could finish my business trip without concern. That was so typical of Nadia; she always took care of everything and told others not to worry. So I flew from Cairo to Brussels on September 2 not knowing that my wife was gravely ill.

The next morning, September 3, I received an e-mail from Shatha: "Urgent. Call us. Mother is sick. The doctor at Shifa wants to transfer her to Israel." I called home immediately. This was no ordinary illness. My Nadia had acute leukemia.

As a physician, I knew this was an ominous diagnosis: most children with acute leukemia survive this cancer of the blood, but only about 50 percent of adults beat the odds. As Nadia's husband, I could only think of what we needed to do to give her a fighting chance. The first step, certainly, was to get her transferred to an Israeli hospital. But even in a life-threatening crisis like this one, crossing the border wasn't easy. She would need a permit to travel. She would also need a commitment from the Palestinian Authority that it would pay for her medical treatment in Israel. It all needed to happen quickly; if chemotherapy for acute leukemia begins immediately, the patient's survival odds improve dramatically. So I got on the phone and called Ramallah to speak to my contacts in the Palestinian Authority. I also asked them to tell the doctors at Al-Shifa to send her to Sheba, the hospital where I worked in Israel.

Thankfully, everyone moved quickly. Nadia's sister-in-law, Aliah, went with her to the Erez Crossing. Of course, my wife stopped off at home on the way to reassure the children that she would be all right and would be back with them soon, and she got into Israel without incident. She could walk without assistance and felt confident that she'd be treated and recover quickly. I shared her confidence. She had always been healthy. The doctors in Israel would know exactly what to do. Frankly, it was inconceivable to me that she could be seriously, ill, and I mentally blocked out any other possibility. I'm sure this is one of the reasons physicians are not supposed to treat members of their own family; they have trouble thinking clinically about the patient and let their emotions enter into their decision making.

My return flight was booked for September 25. Changing the booking would cause enormous complications since all of my travel was based on dated permits. As well, I had a meeting scheduled in Brussels with the European Union to discuss potential employment in the public health field and had planned to stay on an extra two weeks, to visit with colleagues at the Erasme hospital, where I had studied. I was torn: should I try to get home immediately, or should I go to the meeting and return after that? Since her treatment was going well, Nadia suggested I stay in Brussels. She kept saying, "Don't worry." Nonetheless, I should have gone home immediately, and still feel deep anguish and regret over my decision to carry on. I was in part driven by my selfishness in wanting to avoid the paperwork hassle and—even worse—by my personal career interests. I could try to justify my decision by blaming Nadia since she kept saying, "Don't worry. Everything is going fine. I'll see you in a few days." But I know better. I'm the physician and should have done the right thing, which was to rush home to my wife.

It was a horrible few days. It was still Ramadan, and I was fasting. I couldn't sleep for trying to figure out what to do. I kept in daily contact with the family and decided to change my flight to leave Brussels on September 9, immediately after the meeting with the EU. Then I started the tedious and infuriating process of getting the tickets and the permits changed.

I had to go through Amman, which limited my choices, but I managed to find a flight from Brussels to Amman via Munich and Istanbul. It wasn't lost on me that if I wasn't Palestinian, I could have boarded a flight from Brussels to Tel Aviv and been home in a few hours. In the meantime, though, Nadia was responding well to the chemotherapy, and I hoped the worst was behind us; that the terrifying diagnosis had put the wheels of medical intervention into motion and she was on the road to recovery. That was her status when I boarded the plane in Brussels on September 9. By the time the plane landed in Munich later that day, Nadia's condition had taken a sudden turn for the worst and she had been rushed to the intensive care unit. I paced the airport floor, wishing I could somehow transport myself to the Sheba hospital and be by her side. Every time I called, her condition had deteriorated further. I prayed, hoped, begged for her recovery.

It was after midnight when I arrived at the airport in Amman. I found a taxi to take me to the Allenby Bridge, and got there at about two A.M. I'd been traveling since the early morning, sitting in planes, pacing in airports, suffering from that paralytic feeling of having my feet cemented to the floor and my mind in flight to my wife's bedside. But rules are rules, and not even Nadia's worsening condition in a hospital an hour's drive away could alter the hard-hearted fact that the crossing at the bridge would not open until seven thirty A.M. I called to arrange for a driver to wait for me on the other side. I was first in the line waiting for the crossing to open. Mosquitoes buzzed around me, flies irritated me; I couldn't sit down for five long hours as I waited through the night. At last the door to the building opened; I entered, had my papers processed, and was out of there in a matter of minutes. I crossed from the Jordanian side to the Israeli side of the river and was one step closer to Nadia.

That's when my journey to hell intensified—a trip I relive in nightmares. I was first in line at the Israeli security checkpoint. I submitted my passport and identification and was told to wait. At nine o'clock, I was still waiting. At one o'clock, I was still waiting. Other people had arrived, been processed, and left. I beseeched the staff to tell me what was causing the delay. I told them I was a doctor, employed in Israel, explained that my wife was acutely ill, maybe dying, that I'd been traveling for more than twenty-four hours and was desperate to get to the Sheba hospital. The reply? "You have to wait."

I was on the phone every hour with my wife's sister-in-law, who kept saying, "Where are you? Why aren't you here? Hurry, hurry." At two P.M. I'd had all I could handle and started calling friends to ask if they could help. At last I was called up to the counter, where I was told that I had to meet with an officer of the Israeli Security Agency, known in Hebrew as Shabak. He asked me what felt like a hundred questions, and he even asked about my wife. Then he too told me to wait. At six P.M., ten and a half hours after I arrived at this desk, he handed me my passport and told me I could go. The Arab-Israeli taxi driver had waited for me all that time, and I asked him to take me as fast as possible to the Sheba Medical Center. He chose the route with the fewest checkpoints. At the first checkpoint we reached, on the outskirts of Jerusalem, the guard said, "What are you doing here? This is only for Israelis." I explained that I had a permit, that I was a doctor who worked at the Sheba Medical Center in Tel Aviv, that my wife was a patient there and gravely ill, that I was rushing to her side. He behaved as though I were a suicide bomber trying to sneak into the city. He demanded that I turn off my cell phone, then he called the police and told them he'd caught a Palestinian from Gaza trying to cross and that they should arrest me. He insisted I sign a form that said I understood why I was being arrested. Finally a call from Israeli security instructed him to let me go and suggested he should have examined my permit more carefully before sounding the alarm.

You would think the reprimand would have meant something to this man. But all it meant was another delay for me, as he tore up the arrest form he'd filled out and demanded that I sign another paper saying that no one at his checkpoint had harmed me physically. And to prove that he held the trump card, he announced that I had to go to Jericho—over thirty miles back from the checkpoint we were at—and start my return journey all over again. What's more, he instructed me to check in with the director of coordination for Israel in Jericho to get a new permit—mine had now expired.

So we drove with haste to Jericho. Once there, I got the new permit and was instructed to go to the checkpoint in Bethlehem, another detour in my voyage through hell. I was incredulous—but what choice did I have? When we got to Bethlehem, the female soldier in charge entered my name into her computer—and guess what came up on the screen? The same message that had appeared at the Erez Crossing when I had left Gaza on August 16, the same message that had almost canceled my departure, banning me from traveling for security reasons. Since the information had found its way into my file in error, I had presumed it had been removed. Presumption is a wild card in Gaza and the Middle East.

I was sent to a room about three feet by five feet, only enough space to stand up or sit down in, and told to wait. When I heard the key turn in the lock, I could barely contain my rage. It was now half past seven in the evening. My cell phone had been taken away; I could not check on my wife. I sat there power-less while precious minutes of her life ticked by. Each minute felt like a day. The humiliation of being treated as a nobody, a dispensable person, someone who didn't deserve common decency or even the respect of the law, read like a palimpsest of my entire life, the barely erased past being rewritten yet again here in an airless cubicle on the West Bank.

Then one of the officers beckoned to me through the glass wall that separated his desk from where I was being held. Someone unlocked the door, and I proceeded toward this man, who was leaning back in his chair, feet on his desk, finger crooked toward me as if he were calling a dog to sit. He didn't even make eye contact when he thrust the permit toward me and said, "Take it and go."

I was exhausted, hungry, thirsty, and frantic. It took an hour to get to the hospital, and when I finally arrived, I went straight to the intensive care unit. Nadia was unconscious. I called her name, telling her, "I am here with you." I have no idea whether she heard me. Exhausted, I slept on a desk in the hall that night so I wouldn't have to leave her.

The hospital gave me an office space with a bed so I could work and rest. Over the next few days she seemed to improve. Nadia said all along that she would walk on her own feet back to the family. She was absolutely certain that the treatment would make her well. So although it was hard on her and on the children that they couldn't be together, it never occurred to her or to the kids that she wouldn't get back home. As for bringing the children to the hospital, it simply was not allowed; only the patient and one other person were allowed to cross at Erez, and Nadia had come with her sister-in-law. Her doctor even thought she'd be moved out of the intensive care unit soon.

Then suddenly, on Saturday, September 13, her vital signs started to plummet. I knew we were losing her. Our children still couldn't come to see her. Her condition got worse every few hours. She hung on until Tuesday, September 16, at three P.M., when she went into systemic failure and her organs began to shut down. I was sitting beside her, talking to her, calling her name, reading her the Quran. At four forty-five P.M., she slipped away. My wife, the mother of our eight children, was gone.

I couldn't imagine what I would do, how we would cope. Since it was Ramadan and everyone was fasting, I didn't want to call home to tell the children until the fast was broken at a quarter past five that evening. They hadn't had anything to eat all day, and I knew that once they heard about Nadia, they wouldn't eat at all. So I wanted to wait until I was sure they'd had a meal. Instead, I called the Erez Crossing to arrange for a permit for Nadia so that I could bring her body home. Even in death, a Palestinian cannot travel without a permit. Then I called the children. Aya answered the phone. She heard my voice and started to scream. I kept saying to her, "God will compensate us." But all she could say was "No, no, no."

There was paperwork to take care of, an ambulance to hire, a car to arrange for the ride to the border. Once there, it was as though a time machine had caught me. The security screen once again listed me as a risk four weeks after the misinformation was supposed to have been removed, so I could not cross the border with Nadia's body. The Israeli ambulance was to meet the Palestinian ambulance at the vehicle crossing location, and the security officer suggested I let my wife go on in the ambulance and that I complete my paperwork and walk from the Israeli side to the Gaza side. Of course I had done that many times, but I wanted to be by her side for the whole journey home; I did not want my wife to ride alone. I moved through the paperwork as quickly as possible and finally convinced the officer that the restriction on me was an error. I ran though the crossing—at least in the places where running was allowed—and caught up to the ambulance before it reached the Gaza Strip. Nadia and I went the rest of the way home together.

My brothers were waiting. People from all over Gaza had gathered on my street to show their love and sympathy. I went straight to my children, to Bessan, Dalal, and Shatha, to Mayar and Aya, Mohammed, Raffah, and Abdullah.

That night, we all slept together in one room, soothing and gaining strength from each other. The next day, we carried Nadia to the cemetery and buried her there. We prayed all that day and for three more days. Our friends and family came to console us. Our grief was barely manageable, held in check only because we had each other.

Nadia was a wonderful wife and mother, a woman much cherished by our family and friends. I had known her for as long as I could remember. She was my muse. Only by losing her did I fully understand how much I had taken her for granted all these years. I had been able to withstand the chronic frustrations and fears of our lives because Nadia was my support team. With her reassurance and love, I could cope with anything.

My children and I were scarred by her early death, but we are still consoled by our memories of her strength.

SIX

Attack

Nadia's death began a chain of events that altered the lives of my children, changed my career, and challenged my faith.

I stumbled through the fall of 2008, trying to be both mother and father to our children. At first I felt I could not return to work, because my job at the hospital took me away from Gaza from Monday to Thursday every week. Who would take care of the children? On the other hand, if I was without a job, who would take care of any of us?

In my culture, marriage is regarded as the best state of affairs for both men and women. When my wife's sister Maryam came through the tunnels from Egypt to visit her family during Eid, almost four months after Nadia died, I watched the way she hugged and kissed my son Mohammed. Even though he had his sisters, didn't he need a mother figure in his life too? I had never met Maryam, who was divorced and older than me. She had been living in Algeria for decades, and I had been away on her earlier visits. But she wasn't a stranger to my children, and I briefly wondered if I should ask her to marry me. I spoke to her brother about this, and also to Maryam, who said that she was too old for marriage, that she had children and grandchildren of her own.

My children didn't see marriage as a workable solution either. Bessan said, "Go to your work. I will take care of the house.

Dalal and Shatha will help me." It would be a lot for my three eldest daughters: eight children to feed and care for and the large apartment to look after. Bessan and Dalal were students at the Islamic University, and Shatha was in her last year of high school. I talked it over with my brothers, and they said their wives would help. So I decided to go back to work.

Returning to work wasn't a perfect solution, but it did turn out to be a welcome diversion from our grief. The girls worked together to run the house and take care of the younger children while I was in Tel Aviv from Monday to Thursday, and I spent those days at the hospital gratefully absorbed with my patients and the medical issues they brought me. Life without Nadia was not normal, but a semblance of routine had returned to our lives.

In late October 2008, I received a call from Population Services International with the offer of a position in Pakistan. This was my chance to get the family out of Gaza for a while, I thought. The stumbling block was that I had to be either in Dubai or in Pakistan in a couple of days to meet with senior staff, but the Israelis would take at least ten to fifteen days to authorize exit papers from Gaza through the Erez Crossing to Jordan, where I could catch a plane. It looked like it was impossible. Just then, the Palestinians announced that the Rafah border into Egypt would be opened for a couple of days, so I decided to travel through Rafah to get to Jordan so I could catch my flight.

But first I had to provide extensive justification and indisput-able proof to the Interior Ministry of the Hamas government that I needed to travel abroad. (Patients traveling for health reasons, for instance, must present their private medical reports along with their physician's referral; needless to say, patient confidentiality is a nonexistent concept in Gaza. Gazans work-ing outside of Gaza must prove they have a work permit and a visa for that country. Students must submit proof that they are registered at the university abroad.) I was a step ahead of the usual routine this time in that I knew the border was going to be open. Normally, no one has the luxury of deciding when to travel; you wait, prepared to travel whenever the border is open, which could be today, tomorrow, next week, or three, four months from now. I will not enumerate the interminable steps and arbitrary decisions that affect a Palestinian's fate every step of the way across the border. In this case, after twenty-four hours of humiliation, I was one of the lucky ones who made it onto a plane.

After I completed my interviews with PSI in Dubai, of course I wanted to get home to my children as quickly as I could. But how? When? By way of what city and through what crossing? I flew to Cairo and stayed there for a couple of days trying to get a permit and a time to cross, then moved to Al 'Arīsh, about 250 miles from the city and close to the border, so that I could get there as quickly as possible when it opened. My children were on their own, watched over by their aunts and uncles, in our apartment, 55 miles away, a drive of an hour and a half at most.

I had to wait in Al 'Arīsh for about two weeks. I spent the whole time calling everyone I could think of to ask for help simply to return home. One day the Egyptian authorities decided to open the border so that patients who were being treated in Egypt could go back to Gaza, and I was informed that I might also be allowed to pass. I went to the border and begged, explaining that my children were alone, that they recently lost their mother to leukemia, and that they needed their father. But no ears were listening, and no hearts were moved. I waited there all day hoping against hope that human kindness would prevail, but it didn't; I had to return to Al ʿArīsh.

Many people are stranded at the border like I was for days, weeks, even months. Only the well-to-do can take advantage of accommodations available in the nearby Egyptian towns. The others sleep on the ground just outside the border crossing. You can imagine what the sanitation is like in this situation. It is normal to see hundreds of Palestinian travelers waiting to be allowed to cross, including women, old people, young men, and children, all with the same expressions of gloom, frustration, impatience, and fatigue. Traveling has become such a miserable experience that no Palestinian does it, except those who absolutely have to: students attending foreign universities, patients needing care unavailable in Gaza, and businesspeople attempting to pretend that their world will eventually be normal.

As the end of Eid and the Feast of Sacrifice approached, the Egyptians finally allowed me and the others who were stuck at the border to pass. I returned to my children carrying candles, clothes, blankets, food, and kerosene for the stove—items so hard to obtain inside the Gaza Strip.

My absence made me all the more determined to take my family to the olive grove and the beach on December 12, to give us all a break from the endless struggle and our sadness.

That fall, I thought a lot about our future in Gaza and the circumstances surrounding us. Our challenges were personal, yes, but also the saber-rattling between the Israelis and the Palestinians was intense; the tension in the air was so palpable that no one could ignore it, not even Gazans accustomed to tension.

The seeds of this particular impasse were planted after Hamas's election victory, when both Egypt and Israel closed access to Gaza in July 2007. Everything that we needed for survival was controlled by Israel: gas, water, electricity. In retaliation, the United Nations reports, in the seventeen months following the blockade, 2,700 Qassam rockets made in underground labs in Gaza were fired into Israel, killing 4 Israeli civilians and injuring 75 others. During those same months, the Israel Defense Forces hit the Gaza Strip with more than 14,600 artillery shells, which killed 59 Palestinians and wounded 270.

Tension had eased a little in June 2008 after an Egyptian-brokered truce and cease-fire between Hamas and Israel, but then escalated madly again in November. Accusation and counteraccusation seemed the only forms of speech to survive between the Palestinians and Israelis. The blockade had not been lifted during the supposed truce; the borders were never opened. Israeli attacks continued, Qassam rockets flew into Israel, and the IDF killed even more of the so-called militants it found lurking at the border.

The Jewish settlements on the West Bank and in East Jerusalem continued to expand at an ever-increasing rate. Palestinian houses in Gaza continued to be demolished. Land continued to be confiscated; political assassinations escalated. On each side, the habit was to accuse the other side, never examining your own actions. Where was the international community? Who was looking at what was happening to Palestinians? I am against rocket attacks and suicide bombings, but I'm also against shutting the door on people who are suffering, who don't have a chance at a life an ordinary Israeli takes for granted. I ask for a decent life for Palestinians. Instead of building a wall, we need to build a bridge.

On Thursday, December 25, I left the Sheba hospital in Tel Aviv after work and returned as usual to Gaza. The early darkness of a winter evening had settled in, and by the time I got home, the cold damp of the season had seeped into my bones. As I had been winding my way through the checkpoints at the Erez Crossing, Israeli prime minister Ehud Olmert had been issuing what now looks like his final warning to Palestinians in the Gaza Strip, on Al Arabiya television. "I'm telling them now, it may be the last minute; I'm telling them to stop it. We are stronger." Tzipi Livni, the minister of foreign affairs, had also paid a visit to Egypt, which had to be some sort of a sign that action would be taken against the Gaza Strip and the Gazans.

That evening, the children and I discussed the upcoming week and made a grocery list, and on Friday I went to the market to do the weekly shopping. Most people were steeling themselves for the worst, but that day the Israelis suddenly opened two border crossings and allowed more than one hundred truckloads of humanitarian aid to flow into the beleaguered territory, as well as fuel for the power plant. Was it a trick? Did the Israeli government do this so people would let down their guard?

We tried to just take things as they came and get on with life. Our washing machine was broken, so on Saturday morning, after the younger children had gone off to class on the school buses that came for them at six thirty, I drove to Jabalia Camp to get a technician to repair our washer. That's how I came to be away from the house and separated from my children when all hell broke loose in Gaza.

I had just parked and got out of my car when I saw, heard, and felt the attacks begin. It was as if the earth was lifting, shifting, and smashing itself into a different configuration. Israeli rockets, bombs, and shells came from every direction. Bombs fell from the sky. I learned later the Israelis used two-thousand-pound Mark 84 bombs as well as laser-guided penetration bombs. F-16s and Apache attack helicopters roared overhead, rockets ricocheted in from gunships off the coast, and tanks on the border let loose with an astonishing barrage of explosives. The air was full of fire, smoke, and debris. Huge hunks of metal and the remnants of houses mixed with crashing streetlamps and shards of glass.

This first barrage went on for about five minutes. Suddenly it was quiet, the streets dark with destruction. I ran back to my car, which thankfully was still in one piece, and with people screaming in panic all over the roads, I inched my vehicle out of there and found my way home. Bessan was there, but none of the other children. Fear tightened around my chest like a vise. Had they made it to school? Where were they? How would I find them? I'd no sooner formulated a plan to go and search for them than they came through the door, in twos and threes— the younger ones first, then Aya and Mayar from the junior high school, and Shatha from the high school. Dalal had gone to visit her cousin, who was in the same architectural engineering class and lived in another part of the Gaza Strip. I called her on my cell phone. She was there when the shelling began and was safe for the moment, but couldn't get home because the roads were closed.

The children told me that the school buses stopped when the bombing began, and they had decided to try to get home on their own. They would hide during the explosions and run again after they stopped, until they got back to our building. Imagine—schoolchildren having to run for their lives, having to figure out how to get out of harm's way.

December 27, 2008, was the beginning of what would become a twenty-three-day assault on the Gaza Strip. We decided to stay in the apartment because it was the safest place for us; the Israelis knew this was my house, and to me that meant we would never be wrongly targeted in their search for the militants they said they were after. My brother Rezek was in Egypt, so his family left their apartment in our building and went to stay with his wife's parents in Jabalia Camp. My brother Shehab, who lived down the street, decided to send his wife and family to the community center in Jabalia Camp, as they thought it would be safer. Shehab moved in with us so he could keep an eye on his place and also because we'd heard that people living alone were being killed. So, in our building, we had my brother Atta and his family, Nasser and his family, and, in my apartment, the kids and Shehab and me.

By all accounts, this insane attack on the men, women, and children of the Gaza Strip—along with every other living being and anything that humans had built to shelter in—was designed to bring Hamas to its knees, although the official excuse used by the Israelis was that they needed to stop the homemade rocket attacks on Sderot, the Israeli town closest to the Strip, and to end the smuggling of arms into Gaza through the tunnels from Egypt.

I had predicted that this was going to happen sometime and had even stockpiled a few items, such as candles, kerosene, bread, rice, lentils, matches, and any other nonperishables that I could get a hold of—much more than I usually would have done. In Gaza we are living for the moment, and we never know what can happen next. No one, not even the worst pessimist, had imagined that the Israeli attack would go on for twenty-three relentless days. There was no electricity, no phone service, no gas (actually, the gas lines had been cut before the attacks began), and no television. We couldn't sleep for the noise and terror. I went out during daylight hours to scavenge for what we needed to survive, but everything was in short supply. After only a few days, there was no flour to buy and no pita bread, a staple for us, in the stores. Some shopkeepers divided their stock up and prepared baskets, one for each family, but soon enough that was gone as well. Nadia's sister Sobhia heard of a place that had pita. I went with her and my son Mohammed, and between us we managed to purchase three hundred small pitas. With a large extended family, I knew they wouldn't last long.

The ground operation began on January 3. Before that, even though we were under attack, we had been able to move cautiously to the market to get food, but now we became prisoners in our own home. Hundreds of tanks rolled across the border, firing at everything that moved and sending merciless volleys into one building after another. At that point we'd already been under siege for a week. A transistor radio was our only connection to the outside apart from our cell phones, which were now almost out of power although we'd been using them sparingly.

My daughter Shatha and her cousin Ghaida—Atta's daughter, who lived in the same building as us, just one floor away—said they knew how to rig up a homemade charger. To my astonishment these teenage girls connected four radio batteries and turned them into a charger. They cut the cable on the cell phone charger, took the two wires inside the cable and attached one to each end of the batteries, which they had taped together with adhesive, and put the other end of the cable into the phone. It took ten hours to charge one cell phone, but that charger became our lifeline.

The shelling seemed to be coming from every direction. We couldn't figure out who or what the target was. All we ever heard on the radio was the body count, as though we Palestinians had been reduced to numbers rather than mothers and fathers, sisters and brothers.

The dining room, in the center of our apartment, became the sanctuary for the family since we needed to avoid the outside rooms—the kitchen, the bedrooms, and a living room that had wall-to-wall windows and a dangerous exposure to the explosions. I told my children to drag their mattresses into the dining room as we would be safer there and we could all be together. And that's where we stayed, day after day, night after night. We told each other stories. Shatha studied by candlelight because she hoped to be one of the top ten graduates from her high school when the June exams were held. But her choice to study by candlelight wasn't as simple as lighting a candle. We were afraid that the soldiers outside would notice the light and realize there were people inside; we were terrified of making that one lethal wrong move. We took turns hiding the candlelight by whatever means we could. Sometimes we would make a barrier out of cardboard; sometimes we put chairs around the flame; sometimes we used a corner of the wall. My brother Rezek's wife, Aida, kept saying how proud we would all be of Shatha when her studies were completed. I was proud of my family and the way we worked together to survive the horror outside our windows, both physically and psychologically. We offered encouragement and passionate support to each other.

Soon after the assault on the Gaza Strip started, I found myself playing the role of a journalist. Hundreds of correspondents from the international community—BBC, CNN, CBC, Fox News, Sky News—were stuck on a muddy hill outside Ashqelon, the town closest to the Erez Crossing, because the Israeli military refused to allow them access to Gaza. Israeli reporters were refused entry to Gaza as well. Their cameras could capture the plumes of smoke from the exploding bombs, but there were no eyewitnesses from the media to report the facts on the ground. So the Israeli media started calling me on my cell phone since I speak Hebrew fluently and was living in the middle of the catastrophe that their soldiers had created in Gaza.

Shlomi Eldar, my friend from Israeli TV's Channel 10, regularly called me in the late afternoon to ask what had happened that day. From the vantage point of my living room window I could see entire neighborhoods being obliterated with bombs and rockets. And not just one sortie or two; the raids came so often and so powerfully that they reduced the place to rubble, as though to erase the evidence that people had ever lived here—that old people and small children, teenagers, and parents walked on these streets, slept in these houses, ate together, bowed to the east, and kneeled to pray on their mats.

Though I was uneasy at first, worried about reprisals against me and my family, I was finally willing to give these interviews because someone needed to get the story to the outside world. Shlomi later explained why he was calling me: "When the incursion into Gaza started and the media were denied access, I thought he could give us a glimpse into life in Gaza. Starting on the first day of the war, we talked by telephone for four or five minutes during the news portion of the show. He gave us details about how he and his family were coping during the ongoing attack. It was a very unique look at the lives of Palestinians. The audience was not particularly sympathetic as the view of most Israelis was that the Qassam rocket attacks from Hamas into the town of Sderot had to be stopped by any action necessary." Sympathetic or not, with my voice in their ears, Israelis couldn't entirely ignore the costs to Palestinians of their military action.

Living in these surreal circumstances gave me time to think, to project into the future, and to reflect on the past. I knew that eventually the incursion would end, but what then? I'd seen destruction before as a child when Sharon bulldozed our house. Imagine your house being taken from you by force, demolished before your very eyes. How could a person not be in despair or not feel powerless, stripped of dignity, and incapable of differentiating between good and bad? I'd seen further destruction as an adult when the headquarters of the Palestinian Authority was blasted into smithereens by a barrage of shells. How would we ever come back from this lethal attack on the men, women, and children—the innocent civilians of Palestine? How could psychologists, sociologists, medical doctors, and economists rehabilitate the people who had come through the craziness of this annihilation?

As we waited and prayed for deliverance, my thoughts also went to the couples in my fertility clinic who waited every month, praying for good news. Maybe thinking about the anxieties others suffer was a way to keep myself sane, to let my thoughts focus on something other than the present danger to the people I loved. A couple going through fertility treatment also have to wait and hope. It takes a long time. There are the injections given early every morning for a month, the ultrasounds and blood tests, the questions about in vitro fertilization that most couples don't want to discuss when the process begins. There are the unanswered questions, the not knowing.

I remember sitting in the dining room during the barrage thinking about how much these infertile women suffer. I recalled the times I'd had to say, "I'm sorry, the result is negative. You'll have to try again." The words are easy to say but so hard for the woman to hear. Then there are the successful treatments, the joy, the worry, the follow-up, the delivery. Finally, at last there is a baby to love, to raise, to teach. After all that, would this child be huddled on a floor in the middle of the family home trying to avoid a rocket attack? Would all that effort to reproduce lead to fulfilling the dreams of this newborn, or would it lead to a scenario like the one I was sitting in the middle of?

January 13 was the most difficult day of the ground attack thus far. We couldn't see outside because the air was so full of debris and dust from the exploding missiles; you couldn't distinguish day from night. That afternoon there was a loud and persistent knocking at the front door of our apartment building. I didn't want to answer the door for fear it was a soldier daring us to come outside. But the knocking persisted, and finally I descended the three flights and opened the door. My brother Shehab's seventeen-year-old daughter, Noor, was standing on the stoop, holding a white flag over her head, her face wet with tears, her eyes wild with fear. I grabbed her and brought her inside. Her family was still at the community center, but Noor said she couldn't stand to be there any longer. She told us, "There were fifty people in one room. We were packed in like animals and acting like hostages. It was humiliating, embarrassing; there was no privacy whatsoever. I decided I would rather die in my home than stay there." So she wrapped a white towel around a stick and made the dangerous trek to our place.

I felt terrible as I had nothing special to feed my niece to celebrate her courage and to welcome her home. My freezer is always full of food—I'm always prepared to feed however many people come to the door, as is the tradition in my family—but with no electricity, the food had all spoiled. She didn't care. She said, "It's like paradise here because we're all together in the family house."

The next morning, January 14, I saw a tank approaching our building. At first I hoped it had made a wrong turn or was trying to find a space big enough to turn around in. But it came closer and closer. Soon enough it was about ten yards from our door, pointing its guns at the apartment that housed me, my brothers, their wives, and our children. We were waiting—waiting for something, for a miracle—but the time was passing and nothing was happening; yet time was standing still; every moment could have been a minute or an hour; what meaning does time have in situations like this? We had no energy and no power to think. We felt that we were outside this world and that we had no way to face our fate or what the future would bring to us. At that moment, I felt that we had reached the bottommost depths of humanity and that nothing remained ahead of us. What remained was to count on God and our faith. For the three weeks during the war, we lost our belief in humanity, so God and each other were all we had left. Bone-chilling wind was coming through broken windows of the surrounding houses and stores. Children were lying facedown on the street, and they were frozen with fear and anguish. The only other living things on the street were animals—sheep that had strayed from broken pens and were limping along with a leg missing or bullet holes in their sides, donkeys braying pathetically as blood seeped from wounds on their backs. The tank pointing its guns at my house, surrounded by half-dead animals, looked like the angel of death. I called Shlomi Eldar. He later described that phone call.

Izzeldin was shouting, he was clearly very afraid and saying, "There is a tank in front of our house. They're going to kill us, please do something." I didn't know what to do. I called the Israel Defense Forces, but there was no reply. So I called a radio reporter, Gabi Gazit, gave him the details, and said he'd need to go live with the story right away. Izzeldin told his story to him; he was crying on the phone, obviously scared. In the meantime I kept trying to get the IDF on the phone. Taking out Hamas targets was one thing, but attacking the home of a doctor was another. I wanted to make sure they knew whose house they were aiming at.

Once I was connected to Gabi Gazit, we did an interview live on my cell phone, with the tank at my door and the children clinging to me. I felt a colossal, choking fear for my children, a level of terror I had never experienced before. What if they were killed, what would happen to me? What would happen to them if I was killed? The intensity of the situation was like a vice tightening around my forehead. Later Shlomi told me that Gabi was trying to get me to calm down, to be aware of what was going on around me, to be conscious of the details and strong enough for them to broadcast the information clearly and accurately. I really have no memory of the conversation.

Shortly after the interview played on Israeli radio, a military officer called on my cell phone and asked me what was happening. I told him he knew what was happening: an Israeli tank was aiming its guns at my house when only my family was inside. While I stayed on the phone, he called an officer in the field and, as I listened, told that officer to move the tank. Ten minutes later it rolled away. It's hard to believe that only ten minutes had passed. It felt as though it could have been ten days. The crisis was over. I was certain now that we were safe.

We then had an odd sort of celebration. With no gas and no electricity, finding fuel for warmth and for cooking had become a huge issue, but we had a forgotten resource. The day before we went to the beach, I had sent Mohammed to get a bag of charcoal so we could cook our lunch at the olive grove. He misunderstood my instruction to buy two pounds of charcoal, and he bought ten. I was angry with him at the time for not paying attention and spending money needlessly. But now we set up a cooking station outside the apartment door, using that extra charcoal. The children made a cake over the coals, and we boiled water for tea. We felt safe, happy, and for the moment, triumphant.

There was another reason to celebrate despite the danger we were in. That afternoon I had received a call from Dr. Peter Singer and Dr. Abdallah Daar, both professors in the faculty of medicine at the University of Toronto, who urged me to accept a research fellowship there. They had heard about the work I was doing in public health policy and felt I could contribute to the work being done at the university. What started out as a fellowship ultimately became a five-year appointment as associate professor at the Dalla Lana School of Public Health. I had already talked to the children about the potential opportunity to go to Canada, but now I had a firm offer to tell them about. As I look back now at their heartfelt response to the idea of moving to Canada and starting a new life, as I picture their innocent faces looking back at me that late afternoon, I can hardly fathom the event that would alter our lives within forty-eight short hours.

*   *   *

January 15 was a day like all the others during the siege. We couldn't see what was happening outside very well because the air was full of ash. The apartment was beginning to feel crowded; we were ten. Dalal was at her aunt's house, but my other seven children, my brother Shehab, and his daughter Noor were with me. Late that afternoon I lost my temper and told the kids to tidy up their rooms and the rest of the place. The chaos outside was getting to me, and though I was aware that I was taking my anxiety out on them, I couldn't help it. They did as I asked and afterward said they were going to bed. It was only six o'clock but already dark outside as it was wintertime. I knew they were only going to sleep to escape my distressed mood. I felt terrible that I'd upset them and knew I couldn't allow them to go to bed unhappy. So I went to the kitchen and prepared a huge meal of *shakshuka*, made with eggs and tomatoes, which was about all I had left in the pantry—I had bought thirty pounds of tomatoes before the air strikes started—and called them all to come to me from where they were, supposedly sleeping on the dining room floor. They asked why I had been so harsh with them, and I said I was sorry, that it was a mistake on my part to take out the turmoil I was feeling on them.

None of us slept much that night. The sound of the bombing and the rockets penetrated the house, shook our bones. The phone rang at one A.M.; on the line was a man from Israeli radio wanting to do an interview with me. At two thirty it rang again, this time a call from the Jewish Community Center in Pittsburgh, Pennsylvania, asking me to explain what was going on in Gaza. The children heard every word as I replied to the questions and recounted the horror we were living with. I was of two minds about sharing the news with the world and at the same time terrifying my children. The need to alert others to our suffering won out, but the anxiety my graphic descriptions created cost the kids the bit of sleep they might have had that night.

The next morning, January 16, we put the mattresses away and prepared breakfast. Then we discussed what we would eat for the rest of the day, as there was hardly any food of any kind left and there was no way to get to Jabalia Camp, where we always bought our food, because of the intensity of the tank attacks on every street. We couldn't go outside or even approach the windows for fear of the shelling. Though we had barrels on the roof for collecting rainwater, retrieving it was a treacherous task, and we had been rationing water since the attacks had begun on December 27. We only flushed the toilet every few days; no one had taken a shower in two weeks. While we fretted about the food situation, my brother Shehab reminded us that he had ducks in his yard down the street and said he would risk fetching two of them for lunch. Bessan wondered how we would prepare the ducks since we couldn't spare hot water for removing the feathers. Like the issue around recharging the cell phones, we discovered that necessity really is the mother of invention and found a way to skin the ducks, and then served them with rice at about one o'clock that afternoon.

After lunch, we sat together talking about the incursion. The children had dozens of questions: Why would anyone do this to us? When will it stop? What are the leaders saying? I tried to tell them what I knew or had heard through the grapevine over the last few days. I told them that there was talk of a cease-fire. Major General Amos Gilad, the head of the Israeli Defense Ministry's security coordination, was moving back and forth between Egypt and Israel trying to broker a cease-fire. While I was trying to reassure the children that the cease-fire was imminent, my private thoughts took a much darker turn. *These men who meet in the sanctity of safe government offices are not serious about human life and the turmoil here in Gaza. People are dying every minute; every second is vital in saving lives. Women, girls, boys, innocent civilians are being sacrificed for this leadership. Now they're saying a cease-fire will be delayed until January 18. People are not important to the leaders from either side. You have to wonder if they have sons and daughters themselves, and if so, how they could let this happen to anyone's children.*

My son Mohammed asked me why there couldn't be a cease-fire today, right now. He wanted to know more about this man Barak who people said had the power to end the hostilities. My other children, all of us sitting in the circle we'd formed on the dining room floor, asked me about Olmert and what sort of man he is. I had met Ehud Barak at his home in Jerusalem during the Jewish holiday of Sukkoth several years before. There's a tradition during Sukkoth of sending two people from each hospital to bring greetings to the prime minister. When I introduced myself as a Palestinian doctor from the Gaza Strip, Barak asked me to sit beside him; he wanted to know how I became a doctor and how I managed my life coming from Gaza to work in Israel. We sat talking for more than an hour.

I wanted the children to see him as a person rather than as a monster. So I went to my desk to find the photo that had been taken of him with me at that meeting, and another of me with Prime Minister Ehud Olmert, taken when he was the mayor of Jerusalem and had dropped in to the First World Congress on Labor and Delivery. I showed these photos to the children and told them that both men had talked to me about coexistence. But how would I explain that the men smiling beside me in the photos were responsible for the death and destruction outside our windows? How do people forget their humanity and their larger aims? Why do they break their promises? At the back of my mind was another worry: talk of a cease-fire usually also signals the last violent bombardment of the conflict. Invariably the final hours are the most brutal, and when the soldiers retreat, they leave carnage behind.

With the family all around me, this realization was running through my mind like a storm, but I kept a calm face while we talked about our dreams for the future. Bessan told us about her studies at the university and what she hoped to do when she graduated. Mayar had an important announcement: "Aya got her first period this morning. Everyone has to congratulate her on becoming a woman." This is a momentous occasion in a girl's life, and Aya must have keenly felt the loss of her mother, but all of us did our best to reinforce that she'd reached a special stage in her life.

Looking at my children, I was suddenly full of doubt about uprooting them from the life and culture they'd always known. I'd had another recent job offer, this one from Haifa University. I was going to turn it down, but I asked them which they would prefer: to go across the border and live in Haifa or to fly halfway around the world and live in Toronto, Canada. My brothers expressed their view that I should go to Haifa because it would be better to stay close to the extended family, but then Aya repeated her earlier pronouncement, saying, "I want to fly." As we sat there on the floor of the dining room, we agreed that we would go to Canada. My niece Noor said, "Can I come with you? Can you put me in your suitcase?"

We decided we needed to tell Dalal about the family decision to move to Canada; we had been separated since the beginning of the incursion and hardly had a chance to speak with her during all that time. She was excited about the news, but she told us how worried she was about each of us and how she wished we were not apart. We assured her we were all safe and said we were certain this madness would be over soon and we'd be together again. After each of her siblings had spoken with her, I reminded them that my cell phone was our only link to the outside and we needed to save the battery. No one wanted to cut the connection with Dalal, and after we hung up—I remember it was exactly three thirty—we sat together in silence for a long time.

Eventually, we drifted out of the dining room. I needed to prepare for an interview with Oshrat Kotler from Channel 10 about the effect this incursion would have on women's health. Shatha, Mayar, Aya, and Noor went into the bedroom to read, to do homework, to pass the time until we would huddle together again on mattresses spread out on the dining room floor. My older girls' bedroom was big (about sixteen feet by thirteen feet); it had an enclosed balcony and an entire wall of windows. Most of the furnishings in the room had come from trips I had made to other countries: there were bright blue, red, and beige sheets from Egypt and Pakistan and a red Persian carpet from Afghanistan. The ceiling was covered with stars that caught the light all day and shone in the dark at night. Mirrors hung on the walls, and jewelry cluttered their dressing tables, along with Mayar's lip gloss—her latest favorite possession. Dalal's drafting desk, where she created the designs for her study of architecture, sat in one corner of the room. There was a computer on another desk. It occurred to me as I watched the girls from the dining room that despite the shelling and the loss of their mother, there was a level of happiness in this house, a sense of togetherness that stirred my soul.

Raffah was in the kitchen rummaging around for a piece

of bread to make a sandwich, and Bessan was helping her. Mohammed was at the front door, which leads to the staircase of the apartment building, stirring the charcoal to keep the embers going and trying to direct a bit of heat into our cold, damp house. I had finished my preparation for the interview and was playing with Abdullah, carrying him on my shoulders, touring the house, stopping to talk first to Raffah and Bessan in the kitchen, then to Mohammed at the door, and finally entering the girls' bedroom. I was trying to distract Abdullah; at the age of six, the situation was almost incomprehensible to him.

We had left the girls' room and were in the middle of the dining room when it happened. There was a monstrous explosion that seemed to be all around us, and a thundering, fulminating sound that penetrated my body as though it were coming from within me. I remember the sound. I remember the blinding flash. Suddenly it was pitch-dark, there was dust everywhere, something was sucking the air out of me, I was suffocating. Abdullah was still on my shoulders, Raffah came running screaming from the kitchen, Mohammed stood frozen at the front door. As the dust began to settle, I realized the explosion had come from my daughters' bedroom. I put Abdullah down, and Bessan ran ahead of me from the kitchen; we wound up at the bedroom door at the same time. The sight in front of me was something I hope no other person ever has to witness.

Bedroom furniture, schoolbooks, dolls, running shoes, and pieces of wood were splintered in a heap, along with the body parts. Shatha was the only one standing. Her eye was on her cheek, her body covered in bloody puncture wounds, her finger hanging by a thread of skin. I found Mayar's body on the ground; she'd been decapitated. There was brain matter on the ceiling, girls' hands and feet on the floor as if dropped there by some-one who had left in a hurry. Blood spattered the entire room, and arms in familiar sweaters and legs in pants that belonged to these beloved children leaned at crazed angles where they had blown off the torsos. I ran to the front door for help but realized I couldn't go outside because there were soldiers on the street. A second rocket smashed into the room while I was at the door.

To this day I'm not absolutely certain about who was killed when. My brother Nasser had raced down the stairs after the shell hit, and he got to the door at the same time as my brother Atta and his daughter Ghaida. They were caught by the second explosion. I couldn't find Bessan and kept calling her name: "Bessan, Bessan, where are you? Tell me where you are so I can help you." But she was now dead, along with Mayar. So was Aya and so was Noor.

The apartment was full of the dead and wounded. Shatha was standing in front of me, bleeding profusely. I was sure that Ghaida had also been killed as there were wounds on every single part of her body and she lay still on the floor. Nasser had been struck by shrapnel in the back and was also on the floor. I wondered who could help us, who could get us out of this catas-trophe. Then I realized I still had a connection to the outside world. I called Shlomi Eldar, but the call went to his voice mail. I left a message: "YaRabbi, YaRabbi—my God, my God—they shelled my house. They killed my daughters. What have we done?" All I could think was: This is the end. This is the end.

In the meantime, my brother Atta's wife, Sanaa, had attached a white flag to a pole and had left the house to find help. Nasser's wife, Akaaber, went into the street with her. They walked to the refugee camp two and a quarter miles away and told the people there what had happened. Despite the colossal danger in the street, the people from Jabalia all came: our friends and old neighbors, the Palestinians we had grown up with and struggled for survival with. They came with stretchers and blankets, pushing boldly past the soldiers and tanks, to help my family. It took them about fifteen minutes to get to the house.

Meanwhile, I was trying to sort out who else was injured. Shehab had shrapnel in his head and back. I was trying to check his wounds as I held Shatha in my arms, when I looked up to see Mohammed, and was stricken by the thought that he had just lost his mother and now three of his sisters were gone. I did not realize that tears were streaming down my face. All I know is that my thirteen-year-old son saw the state I was in and gave me a precious gift. He told me not to be sad, that his sisters were happy and with their mother. He meant this; it came from the depths of his faith. Then Mohammed said, "Ghaida took a breath." Before that I thought she too was dead, but he was right. My old neighbors lifted Shatha, Ghaida, Nasser, and Shehab onto stretchers and wrapped the bodies of Bessan, Mayar, Aya, and Noor in blankets, and we set out to carry them to the hospital.

We kept walking. My mind was racing. I knew that if Ghaida had any hope of surviving her wounds and if Shatha's eyesight could be saved, we needed to get to an Israeli hospital, but we were walking to the Kamal Edwan hospital in northern Gaza, which with thousands of casualties to treat had long ago run out of the equipment the medical staff would need to help my daughter, my niece, and my brothers. When we arrived there, I called Shlomi again.

Shlomi picks up the story from here.

It was five on Friday afternoon, and I was doing the news when I saw Izzeldin's name come up on the screen of my mobile phone. I was live on air so didn't answer the call. But I wondered what was going on. We were about to do an interview with Foreign Minister Tzipi Livni, and the introduction had already begun when I saw his name come up on my mobile again and I made the decision to take the call live on air. I told the viewing audience that we had something very important coming in and pushed the telephone speaker button and held the mobile phone up so the viewer could see it. I think my director wondered what on earth I was doing taking a phone call in the middle of a live news broadcast.

Izzeldin was incredibly distraught and repeated what I heard later on my voice mail: "They shelled my house. They killed my daughters. What have we done?" I can't tell you how extraordinary this was—it's not something a news anchor ever does—to take a call in the middle of the show. I was all the time wondering if this was the wrong thing to do at the same time as I was listening in abject horror to what he was saying. Then I heard my editor's voice in my earpiece saying, "Move the telephone closer to the microphone."

The conversation that followed was heartbreaking. He kept crying, "Oh God, they killed my daughters. Shlomi, I wanted to save them, but they are dead. They were hit in the head. They died on the spot. Allah, what have we done to them? Oh God." His surviving children were screaming in the background when I asked Izzeldin where he lived. He was sobbing. "No one can get to us. Oh Shlomi, oh god, oh Allah, my daughters are dead." He told me the roads were closed and that they couldn't move toward the border. I asked him which junction his house was near. He told me, and I said on air, "If anyone hears us in the IDF, call the Zimmo junction. Maybe some of the wounded can still be saved." I wondered if we could ask for a cease-fire and get an ambulance to come. All this was live on air.

Frankly, I don't know what made me decide to push that telephone button. Was it instinct for news? Was it my heart speaking louder than my head?

Once I'd heard Izzeldin begging for help, pleading that we get ambulances to the border, I knew I couldn't leave the story. I said to the viewing audience, "I don't know how I can hang up this phone, so I will excuse myself from the studio, because I cannot hang up on him." I took off my microphone, got up from the anchor desk, and walked to my office to make a phone call to the administrator of the Erez checkpoint. I shouted at him to please open the border and get them out of Gaza to the hospital and let the ambulances we'd called through. My producer sent a cameraman to follow my movement to the office. In the meantime, a military correspondent from our channel was calling every soldier he knew and asking them to help.

The live part—that's the clip that shot around the world on YouTube—went on for between five and seven minutes. But I didn't want to cut my telephone connection with Izzeldin, so I stayed on the line with him until the ambulances arrived at the border. My producer had sent my cameraman to the border, and he picked up the footage of the story there.

When I got Shlomi on the phone, he said, "Ambulances are coming from this side, and we are working to make sure there is permission for the Palestinian ambulances to move to the Erez Crossing and make the transfer."

I hung up and was moving toward the border with the ambulances from Kamal Edwan hospital when Dr. Zeev Rotstein, the director general of the Sheba Medical Center, phoned to say he had heard the terrible news. He told me to come immediately with the two wounded children and my brother Nasser (Shehab stayed behind for treatment at Kamal Edwan) to the Sheba hospital, that he would arrange everything. He was the voice of reason in the midst of madness, chaos, and indescribable grief.

As the ambulances headed toward the Erez Crossing, bombs were still dropping, rockets whizzing through the streets, people screaming. But it was surreal—I had no fear at all. It was as though I had moved emotionally into an untouchable zone: the worst had already happened, and nothing could frighten me now. Mohammed had taken Raffah and Abdullah to his aunt's house, where Dalal was staying, and that's how she found out that Bessan, Mayar, Aya, and Noor had been killed and that Shatha and her cousin Ghaida were gravely wounded. My brother Atta stayed with them while we inched our way across the border into Israel.

Just as Shlomi had promised, there were ambulances waiting on the other side, but Ghaida was dying, and I didn't think she would survive the trip in the ambulance all the way to Sheba hospital. She needed a helicopter, but the crossing was a military zone and no helicopter was allowed to land there. So I sent her to Barzilai hospital in nearby Ashqelon, which wasn't equipped to treat her severe head wound but could give her blood and stabilize her, and most important, it was a place where a medical helicopter could land. I went with my daughter and brother in the ambulances to Sheba while Ghaida was taken by ambulance to the Barzilai hospital. Soon enough, all of us arrived at Sheba—Ghaida airlifted from Ashqelon—to an enormous show of support from the staff I'd worked with, as well as passionate blessings from Arab, Muslim, Jewish, and Christian people in Israel who had been watching the drama unfold on television and had gathered in the hospital foyer to wait for us.

It was after midnight when Shlomi came from the studio to talk to me. He was shocked to see me still covered with blood and wanted to know what more he could do for my family. He had already done more than anyone could possibly ask. He'd masterminded the rescue that probably saved the life of my niece Ghaida and the eyesight of my daughter Shatha.

Back in Gaza, Dalal was having to cope with the terrible news and take care of the younger children. She said later that she was so grateful for the telephone call just before the shells hit: "It was like a conference call—we were all talking at once. I remember I said to Bessan and Aya, 'This is the first time I had a chance to talk to everyone together.' They were so important to me. Bessan, Shatha, and I were best friends. Bessan and I were always together at the university. That's why I was crying when I asked her, 'Are you safe?' She told me she was safe, but she wasn't. Not at all. My pain in this loss is too great. I can't stay in Gaza. I can't stay in our house anymore. I can't go back to the university."

In the meantime, Dr. Rotstein was on the phone in Tel Aviv. He remembers the details of that day and the ones that followed much better than I do, so I'll let him describe what happened:

> I wanted to bring the rest of his family here to Israel. It was the humanitarian thing to do regardless of what was going on. I hoped to create a small haven in this global hell for them. I couldn't bear the idea that after the horrible disaster, part of the family was there and part here, that there was a split amongst the surviving children. They needed to be united.

When I met with Izzeldin the next morning at the hospital, I was totally lost for words; I hadn't any idea what to say to him. But instead of me finding the words to encourage him, I found myself being encouraged by him. His message was that his own personal disaster should serve as a kind of milestone, and from here we should do more for peace in order to prevent such a horrible thing from happening again.

At the same time he was trying to establish that the Israeli army had made a mistake, and I agreed with him. If the rockets had been fired accidentally, the army should admit that. I told him, "I can assure you, there won't be a cover-up." He kept saying over and over again, "I want the truth. Nothing can bring my daughters back, but I have to know the truth." I vowed I wasn't going to let this go. I spoke to a senior army chief of staff and said that Izzeldin Abuelaish was one of my team members, part of my staff. I was promised that the army would get to the bottom of it. Eventually they did admit that the shelling of the doctor's house had been a terrible mistake.

That same morning I held an improvised press conference and asked Izzeldin to speak. To be honest, my attempt was not well received. Some felt that as a government employee I had no right to invite him to the podium. We try to avoid politics. We do humanitarian work. But that shouldn't stop us from facilitating the conversation where what needs to be said is said. I was attacked afterwards, mostly by the families of Israeli soldiers, because every single thing here that relates to Israel or Palestine is terribly sensitive. However, my feeling is that I'm not just a manager or an administrator, I'm a leader, and I'm obliged to contribute vision and beliefs rather than simply execute instructions. Even without declaring what I felt, I should lead rather than be led.

During the press conference, an Israeli woman interrupted the proceedings to claim that my house was targeted because I was harboring militants. Levana Stern, the Israeli mother of three sons, one of whom was with the IDF in Gaza, tried to blame me for the tragedy, screaming at me, saying I must have been hiding weapons in my home or that some Hamas soldiers must have found a safe haven in my house so they could fire at the Israeli soldiers. When I stood up to refute these accusations, Ghaida was upstairs in the intensive care unit in critical condition with shrapnel wounds all over her body, and Shatha had come out of the surgery that would restore her eyesight and reattach her middle finger and was resting in a room upstairs.

I felt as though my family had been re-attacked, as though my daughters and niece had been killed all over again by this dishonest version of the murderous event. It was so painful to hear the truth falsified. One person in the lobby who was watching the press conference even dared to suggest my girls were killed by Qassam rockets fired at them by Hamas.

From the moment we arrived in the hospital, I was thoroughly committed to finding out how this had happened, and I now realized a cover-up was a real possibility. I wanted the Israeli army to tell me why my home, which had harbored no militants, which was filled with children whose only weapons were love, hopes, and dreams, was fired upon. I expected an apology from the IDF. I felt certain they would say that an errant tank shell had hit my home. But in the days after the attack, that's not what I heard. First, the excuse was that there were snipers on our roof. But if there were snipers on the roof, why had they fired twice at the third floor of a five-story building? Then, that pieces of shrapnel taken from Ghaida's wounds were actually fragments of a Qassam rocket, which was not true. Then came variations on Levana Stern's charges: the Israeli soldiers were firing at militants in my house. But the only militants I harbored were my children, who were militant about love, hope, and dreams. An army spokesperson said a preliminary investigation showed that soldiers were returning fire in the direction of a building from which they'd been fired upon. One army officer said, "The Israel Defense Forces does not target innocents or civilians, and during the operation into Gaza the army has been fighting an enemy that does not hesitate to fire from within civilian targets."

I was outraged by the remark. These are very sophisticated weapons, and the IDF know precisely what they have targeted. In this case, they had set their sights on a girls' bedroom. All that was ever fired out of our house was love, hugs, and acts of peace—nothing else, ever. It was immoral to, in effect, stab four children with lies after they were already dead.

When I was interviewed on TV about what happened, I was also asked what I thought about Levana Stern. I said that I would like to meet her one-on-one and that I would listen to her if she would listen to me. The media arranged the meeting, but she arrived with a cold and distant attitude, and although she told others in the room that she was sorry for my loss—and did apologize to me later—she insisted that she still believed Israel had fought this war to defend itself. A Tel Aviv weekly newspaper put it another way when it wrote: "Levana Stern didn't attack Abuelaish. She was protecting herself from him because he threatened her view of Palestinians as terrorists."

Then an Israeli official was quoted as saying that I should have left my home before my children were killed. But where were we to go? Mosques, schools—every place was a target. I even sought advice from my Israeli friends, including Shlomi

Eldar. They told me it was best to stay home and keep a low profile. There wasn't one safe place in Gaza. So I stayed at home because I believed that everyone knew which house was mine and because I felt it was the safest place for my family. Besides, there was no reason to leave because I was not in the line of fire from either side.

The fact is, Israeli tanks were moving from house to house, shelling and destroying homes they said were thought to serve as Hamas positions. By the look of the streets of Gaza in the aftermath, you could be forgiven for thinking that every single home must have been a hideout for armed Hamas soldiers. Everyone on both sides knows that this is absolute nonsense, and I believe the Israeli soldiers were driven into overkill by groundless fear fostered by so many years of hostilities and prejudice. The troops' actions even led some of the hard-nosed military supporters within Israel to criticize the IDF for using excessive force.

Following the attack, my friends surrounded me in the lobby of the hospital, where we gathered every day, usually after I had done one media interview or another. People I had never met also came to show their support for me and their dismay with the military, and some others came to assert that my daughters and niece were merely a casualty of war. Tammie Ronen, a professor of social work at Tel Aviv University, had been working with me to research the effects of conflict-related stress on Palestinian children in Gaza and Israeli children in Sderot, the border town that has been hit by rocket fire during the last eight years. She said, "You cannot let yourself collapse. You have your living children to take care of." I saw Anael Harpaz coming toward me. She had been upstairs with Shatha, holding her hand while the nurses administered pain medication, and now she was here to support me. Anael is the woman who met my children Bessan, Dalal, and Shatha at the Creativity for Peace camp in Santa Fe, New Mexico. I called out to her and said, "Tell these people who my children were." She was sobbing and saying, "I hope this is a wake-up call. This is such a peace-loving family."

While I watched over Shatha, Ghaida, and my brother in the hospital in Tel Aviv, my three daughters and niece were buried in Gaza. The Quran says the deceased must be buried quickly, and it was impossible for me to get a permit to cross the border in time to be there for them. Even in death we are separated from our beloved ones. And in one more breathtakingly cruel addition to this tragedy, I was told that Bessan, Mayar, and Aya couldn't be buried beside their mother because the Israeli soldiers said no one was allowed to go into that area. Their graves are a few miles away from the Jabalia Camp cemetery where Nadia is buried.

Revenge was on the lips and in the minds of most people I talked to in the days after my daughters and niece were killed. Zeev Rotstein had managed to bring my other children to Tel Aviv and arranged lodgings for all of us near the hospital. Atta, who had been taking care of my younger children and arranging the funeral for the girls, came too. His daughter Ghaida remained in intensive care with wounds so severe we wondered if she would survive. Shatha needed more surgery to save her eyesight. I remember after one of the operations, Dalal passed chocolates around to the staff and other patients in the hospital; it's our way of marking a blessed event. We struggled together, my children and I, and I tried to respond to the chorus of people calling for Israeli blood to atone for the deaths of my girls. One said, "Don't you hate the Israelis?" Which Israelis am I supposed to hate? I replied. The doctors and nurses I work with? The ones who are trying to save Ghaida's life and Shatha's eyesight? The babies I have delivered? Families like the Madmoonys who gave me work and shelter when I was a kid?

Still, the cries for reprisals didn't stop. What about the soldier who fired the deadly volleys from the tank? Didn't I hate him? But that's how the system works here: we use hatred and blame to avoid the reality that eventually we need to come together. As for the soldier who shelled my house, I believe that in his conscience he has already punished himself, that he is asking himself, "What have I done?" And even if he doesn't think that now, tomorrow he will be a father. He will suffer for his actions when he sees how precious is the life of his child.

To those who seek retaliation, I say, even if I got revenge on all the Israeli people, would it bring my daughters back? Hatred is an illness. It prevents healing and peace.

Shlomi Eldar told me later that our few minutes together on television had left an indelible impression on his viewers. He said: "The broadcast had a huge effect on Israelis who until then didn't want to hear about anything from Gaza because they were so angry about the eight years of rockets being fired into Israel by Hamas. The majority of Israelis were in favor of the incursion. Now, for the first time, they understood what was happening inside Gaza. I'm told it was Izzeldin's voice and my face that made the story. I was very close to crying as I listened to his agony. That same agony affected the Israelis who were watching the program. Even the prime minister of Israel told me he was crying when he saw this on TV. It wasn't prime time, but even six and seven months later people told me they saw it live on TV. I believe those five or seven minutes of television led to the cease-fire.

"Part of the story that fascinated me was the way Izzeldin moved back and forth between being a father and a physician—at one moment weeping about the tragedy, at another demanding his daughter and niece and brother be taken to the Sheba hospital because there were better facilities to treat them there."

As much as I reached for calm and a larger mission during those terribly dark hours, my thoughts kept drifting back to the girls—those beautiful, innocent daughters and niece of mine. I sat in the hospital, imagining their futures, their weddings, the contributions they would have made to the world. And I thought about how a dream of happiness can turn into a nightmare in a matter of seconds. A person you've nurtured for years is lost to you in a flash of destruction. It felt as though they had been kidnapped from me.

I longed for the day to be replayed: they wouldn't have been in the bedroom; the rumored cease-fire would have already been in place. But I also tried to focus on the survivors and how I could help them recover. I looked at it as a believer: God had given me my daughters as a trust, and now they were taken back. But I was also consumed with the craziness of this act, the blind stupidity of attacking the citizens of Gaza and claiming the rampage was aimed at stopping the rockets being fired into Israel.

School started again at the end of January, and so after they stayed with me for ten days, I sent the children back to Gaza to stay with my siblings. Raffah was haunted by nightmares and even wet her bed, and Mohammed was troubled so deeply he suffered seizures for months after his sisters were killed.

Abdullah, the baby of the family, the one who was out of diapers by the time he was a year old, started to wet himself and his bed again. He was so upset by this bed-wetting that he insisted someone else had done it and it couldn't have been him. During those long days, while my daughter, niece, and brother recovered, and before I was able to return to our smashed, empty, sad home in Gaza, my overriding questions were: Why did this happen to us? And what am I going to do about it?

SEVEN

Aftermath

The aftermath of the shelling of our house continued to be tumultuous. I can hardly sort out the threads: the agony of loss; the flood of e-mails and handwritten letters from people around the world, most of them strangers who wanted to reach out to my family and share our sorrow; the extraordinary support of my colleagues; the cease-fire that came two days too late, on January 18; the questioning faces of my surviving children. Now what? What am I to do to make sense of this?

On April 1, I left the small apartment where I stayed near the Sheba hospital and brought Shatha home. We were greeted on the Palestinian side of the Erez Crossing by a crowd of our relatives and friends bearing flowers and the Palestinian flag. Busloads of students, neighbors, professors, and doctors also arrived, even the president; the media showed up to film our return, and there were hugs, kisses, and speeches and destruction all around us. Nasser had recovered from his injuries and had gone home three weeks after the tragedy. Ghaida, who was still healing, stayed on in the hospital in Israel for two more weeks before she was well enough to come home. Construction workers had begun to repair and rebuild the remnants of the bedroom where my daughters and niece died; building materials were hard to find, and the prices had quadrupled. Despite the incessant hammering, sawing, scraping, and pounding of the workers' tools, my house seemed deathly quiet. I was determined to sleep in my own bedroom, but my children stayed on with my brothers Atta and Rezek, and with my sisters Etimad and Yousra; they tried so hard to be brave, but their barely concealed anguish was difficult to bear. One night I found a poem on my pillow—a message to Aya written by Raffah. Translated, it reads:

No no no—where did you disappear to from our home
Aya, you were the light of our home
What's happened to the home that was lit up by you
Where has the beautiful light gone
Where has the beautiful girl gone
No no no.
Where have you disappeared Aya

What do you say to a child who writes such words? And Mohammed kept repeating, like a prayer, "The girls are with our mother. They are happy there. My mom asked for them."

What if I had been at the hospital in Tel Aviv when the attack began? I would have been separated from the children for the duration of the incursion, unable to care for them, receiving the dreadful news at a distance.

I had always worried that something catastrophic would happen to my family when I was away from them. As a boy, I feared something would happen to my mother, and after we married, I worried for Nadia, especially when my training and work kept taking me out of the country. I realized in the aftermath that I was grateful that neither my mother nor Nadia had witnessed this disaster.

The personal aftershocks of our loss kept rippling out. Ghaida had been so critically wounded that for a time we couldn't risk telling her that Bessan, Mayar, Aya, and Noor were all dead. When she asked for the girls, we told her they were also wounded, also in critical care. For a while such evasions did soothe her, although she'd say things like, "Just don't tell me they died." She kept asking, of course, and finally we—her father, Shatha, and I—knew it was time for her to be told. Shatha was the one who did it. She held her cousin's hands and explained that all four girls had died in the attack. Ghaida started screaming and shouting that she never wanted to go home again, that if her cousins weren't there, she never wanted to be in our apartment again. We were so worried we'd made a mistake; she was still in serious condition. But Shatha stayed with her, and eventually they brought comfort to each other, these teenage survivors who were dealing with shrapnel and stitches, pain and loss.

From the moment we got home—with smashed buildings, collapsed bridges, and rubble all around us—I realized that I had two options to choose from: I could take the path of darkness or the path of light. If I chose the path of darkness, of poisonous hate and revenge, it would be like choosing to fall into the complications and the depression that come with disease. To choose the path of light, I had to focus on the future and my children.

But first, there were some truths that had to be addressed. The Gaza Strip was wrecked—bombed to pieces. It wasn't just the government buildings and police headquarters, which the Israel Defense Forces had insisted were the targets, but entire neighborhoods that had nothing whatsoever to do with political parties or militants. From the window of my house, as far as I could see, there was the disgraceful sight of a scorched-earth policy fulfilled. In Jabalia City alone there was some five hundred thousand tons of rubble; it looked like a cross between Sarajevo under siege and Afghanistan after the mujahideen were finished with it. The burned-out apartment buildings, the blackened shells that once were houses, the gaping holes where windows had been that made the buildings still standing look like ghosts—it was all a testament to the overkill that comes with the hatred engendered by engaging in war. That's the thing about war: it's never enough to disable the buildings, to blow holes into their middles; instead, they're hit over and over again, as if to pound them to dust, to disintegrate them, to remove them from the earth, to deny that families ever lived in them. But people did live there. And they needed to return, even though there was nothing left to return to except forbidding piles of broken concrete and cable wires sticking out of the heaps like markers of malevolence.

When I surveyed the wanton destruction, I couldn't help but ask myself what on earth the soldiers thought they were doing. Who made these decisions? What were they thinking when they did this? The IDF speaks about Qassam rockets; who was going to speak about this?

As it turned out, a lot of people had a lot to say about what went on in Gaza during those dreadful winter days. It was dubbed the Gaza War in the mainstream media, code-named Operation Cast Lead by the IDF, called the Gaza Massacre in the Arab world and the War in the South by the Israelis. The reports of how many were killed are inexact, but everyone on all sides agrees that the number is between 1,166 and 1,417 Palestinians and 13 Israelis. There are more statistics to cite among the living: more than 400,000 people in Gaza were left without running water; 4,000 family homes were destroyed or so badly damaged the people couldn't return; tens of thousands became homeless; eighty government buildings were bombed.

In September 2009, the United Nations Human Rights Council released a report on the incursion, and a new firestorm ensued—this one of words—from the political arms of both sides, condemning the report, which had been written by the respected South African judge Richard Goldstone. He called the Israeli assault on Gaza "a deliberately disproportionate attack designed to punish, humiliate and terrorize a civilian population." He accused the Israeli military of carrying out direct attacks against civilians, including shooting civilians who were trying to leave their homes to walk to a safer place, waving white flags. He blamed the IDF for the destruction of food production and of water and sewerage facilities, and he accused them of being systematically reckless with their use of white phosphorus while bombing Gaza City and the Jabalia refugee camp, of attacking hospitals and UN facilities, and of rocketing a mosque during prayers.

But he also criticized Hamas for firing eight thousand rockets into Israel over the last eight years, calculated to kill civilians and damage civilian structures. The report accused Palestinian armed groups of causing psychological trauma to the civilians within the range of the rockets, hitting Israeli houses, schools, and a synagogue, and forcing civilians to flee. Judge Goldstone called for a public inquiry on both sides, but his pleas fell on deaf ears. The Israeli government described the report as full of "propaganda and bias," and Hamas said it was "political, imbalanced and dishonest."

That's how things happen in the Middle East—the size of the rhetoric trumps the facts on the ground. In my experience, the vast majority of Israelis and Palestinians were horrified by the terrifying events of the three-week war. The reaction of ordinary people strengthens the case for our need to talk to each other, to listen, to act. And it reinforces my lifelong belief that out of bad comes something good. Maybe now I really have to believe that; the alternative is too dark to consider. My three precious daughters and my niece are dead. Revenge, a disorder that is endemic in the Middle East, won't get them back for me. It is important to feel anger in the wake of events like this; anger that signals that you do not accept what has happened, that spurs you to make a difference. But you have to choose not to spiral into hate. All the desire for revenge and hatred does is drive away wisdom, increase sorrow, and prolong strife. The potential good that could come out of this soul-searing bad is that together we might bridge the fractious divide that has kept us apart for six decades.

This catastrophe of the deaths of my daughters and niece has strengthened my thinking, deepened my belief about how to bridge the divide. I understand down to my bones that violence is futile. It is a waste of time, lives, and resources, and has been proven only to beget more violence. It does not work. It just perpetuates a vicious cycle. There's only one way to bridge the divide, to live together, to realize the goals of two peoples: we have to find the light to guide us to our goal. I'm not talking about the light of religious faith here, but light as a symbol of truth. The light that allows you to see, to clear away the fog— to find wisdom. To find the light of truth, you have to talk to, listen to, and respect each other. Instead of wasting energy on hatred, use it to open your eyes and see what's really going on. Surely, if we can see the truth, we can live side by side.

I am a physician, and as a consequence I see things most clearly in medical terms. I am arguing that we need an immunization program, one that injects people with respect, dignity, and equality, one that inoculates them against hatred.

I have dedicated my life to peace, to healing, to bringing babies into the world, to solving the problems of the infertile. My work involves doing joint research projects with Israeli physicians; for years I've been something of a one-man task force bringing injured and ailing Gazans for treatment in Israel. This is the path I believed in and what I raised and educated my children to believe in. I find it incomprehensible that after a lifetime of contributing all I had to coexistence, I should be the one to bear witness to the worst consequences of war.

The New York columnist Mona Eltahawy interviewed me about six weeks after the tragedy. She wrote, "He seems to be the only person left in this small slice of the Middle East with its supersized servings of 'us' and 'them' who refuses to hate." She was making a point that's important to me. I don't spend time feeling sorry for myself and I certainly don't hate anyone, but I have wondered why this happened to me. Why was I spared when my daughters were killed? Was I selected for a reason? Many people, both friends and strangers, have remarked on the dual tragedies that have been visited on my family during the last year—the sudden death of Nadia, the loss of my daughters and niece—and they ask if I feel like I'm being punished. I don't. But I do wonder at times why I was not the one to die.

I sometimes feel like Ayoub in the Quran or Job in the Talmud and the Bible: the man whose faith in God was so severely tested. His crops were destroyed, his children were killed, he suffered from disease and loss of wealth, his friends abandoned him, but he still kept his faith. I've been tested, and I have the feeling that I'm expected to come up with a solution.

As a believer, I feel that I have been chosen to reveal the secrets of Gaza, the truth about the pain of the dislocation, the humiliation of the occupation, and the suffocation that comes from a siege, so that once and for all Palestinians and Israelis can find a way to live side by side.

I believe in coexistence, not endless cycles of revenge and retribution. And possibly the hidden truth about Gaza can only sink in when it is conveyed by someone who does not hate. I've been tested by brutal circumstances the whole of my life, as have many people in Gaza. Until now I have seen each hardship as an opportunity to make myself stronger, as an energizer that propels me forward, as a weapon so as to be better armed for the next struggle, but maybe the tests have been designed to strengthen me as a messenger who can help bridge the divide in the Middle East.

I am not a prophet; I'm a human being and a believer who is trying to accept that what happened to my family was God's plan. The perpetrator was man, the violence man-made, but surely my mission is to try my hardest to ensure that the consequences lead to good, not to ever-increasing evil, violence, and despair.

I believe everything happens for a reason, and that even my family's terrible loss serves a purpose. The deaths of my daughters and niece opened the Israelis' eyes to the suffering on the other side. That's the message I want to spread: allow yourself to see what it's like to be in our shoes. The tragedy certainly led to the cease-fire and opened the hearts and minds of the Israeli public, the whole Palestinian diaspora, and the international community to the misery the Gazans face day after day. I believe that there is a better future for us because of what this tragedy taught the world. There is hope; the past is only there to learn from.

*   *   *

Anael Harpaz, the Israeli woman who met my daughters Bessan, Dalal, and Shatha at the peace camp in Santa Fe, came to visit Shatha and me in the hospital and ended up staying by Shatha's side for the entire ten weeks she was there. At the end of March, just before we were to move back to Jabalia, she sent me an e-mail whose subject line was "In Memory of Bessan." It read:

Hi Beloveds ... at long last I have time now to mourn for Bessan. Before I was too busy and needed to be strong and present for Shatha and Ghaida, her cousin—the flood gates of tears have opened and with this a poem that always helps me to process and feel better afterwards. Thank each and every one of you for your commitment to peace. May Bessan's death be the foundation for deep change and may all people in this region know what we know in our hearts. Sending you all much love. If any of you have written something that you would like to share about this difficult time or about Bessan—please send it to me. Someone has volunteered to do a website in memory of the girls and we would like stories, poems or anything that you feel would be appropriate. Here's my poem:

> ### Where Love Resides . . .
> in memory of Bessan
>
> I long to touch you Bessan
> One more time
> To hug you
> To tell you how sorry I am
> that your mom died
>
> But now you too are gone.
> Your smiling face

Your gentle way
Your softness
Your non-judgmental words
Your pain for your people
Your way of life
Your dreams, aspirations
and your hope for peace
Just days before the war
I spoke with your dad
He gave me your phone number
It is still in my car
Every day
I glance at the number
seeing your name
Bessan
I wish I had spoken with you more
but I didn't have the guts
I spoke with you three days before you died
I told you that I am praying for your safety
My prayers were not heard
through the shelling
the bombing
the Qassams
the smoke
I feel I have been betrayed by God
By my country
By the cruelty of humanity
By the warmongers
By those who think violence is the solution
And with all of this
I have been given a gift

To have spent six weeks
with Shatha, Izzeldin,
Atta and Ghaida
I heard no words of revenge
nor hatred
I heard no anger I heard the deep belief
that peace is possible
even with this enormous loss
I have been strengthened
from their strength
I am more determined
from their determination
I am more at peace
from their peacefulness
Bessan forgive me
for not being able to save you
from my own people
Forgive me for giving you hope
that peace is possible
and then taking that dream from you
You will always be my symbol
of hope, peace and mostly
gentleness
Your dad shared a dream with me
days after you died.
He came into a room full of men
and there you were
sitting amongst them
He asked you
"Why are you sitting here?
You know it is not acceptable in our society"

You answered
"All is fine now Dad
I am happy and well.
I can be here now among the men where I am
needed."
May no other woman need to die
in order to be able to influence
the men as you have Bessan.
May we women
be heard and heeded
and may the men in this world
get the chance to know from deep within their
hearts that this is where the answer lies
In their hearts
where love resides.

Anael—March 2009

Her words struck a major chord with me. I am presently laying the groundwork for a foundation in honor of Bessan, Mayar, and Aya, whose aim is to empower women and girls through health and education programs in order to promote change for women and girls throughout the Middle East. As I have written earlier, women in this region have not been part of the discussion in civil society, but Palestinian women know about sacrifice and suffering. They know how to manage in the face of chaos. It's not that the women aren't able to participate; the issue is that they've been denied the right to take part in discussions vital to our future.

I want to see that opportunity come to women and girls everywhere. I want them to be part of the conversation. I've been delivering Palestinian babies and Israeli babies for most of my working life. There's no difference between a Palestinian newborn and an Israeli newborn, and I believe that the mothers who give birth to these babies can find the way forward for this region.

Many women and girls in Gaza cannot get an education because of their financial and cultural circumstances. I firmly believe that Palestinian women can carry the torch of change into the future, but first they need to be released from the bondage that culture, occupation, siege, and suffering have imposed upon them. Empowerment means being independent and respected, and to create change in an entire society, women must be educated and empowered.

Part of the aftermath of this tragedy is that I've had the opportunity to travel even more widely to countries in Europe, North America, and Asia to speak on coexistence and the real truths of Gaza. Each visit presents me with a chance to represent the facts accurately, to right the wrongs, and to gain supporters for coexistence and human rights in the Middle East—and everywhere else. At the same time, I talk about the lives of women and the work my foundation plans to do. My stand on coexistence has set me apart, but now that I am challenging the status of women in the Middle East, I have two platforms to speak from.

I was invited to Brussels in April 2009 to meet members of the European Parliament. While I was there, I was awarded honorary Belgian citizenship and given the opportunity to meet with the president of the EU Parliament, Hans-Gert Pöttering of Germany. I also found out that Jean-Marc Delizée, secretary of state for the Belgian Parliament, had nominated me for the Nobel Peace Prize for 2010. I spoke to the media that day in order to dedicate the nomination to people everywhere who suffer from prejudice and injustice, and to the leaders of both the Israeli and Palestinian peoples, urging them to work together to prevent further destruction and pain. Enough blood, enough animosity! Military means have proven a failure, and a new method must be found to deal with the conflict. We must focus now on the lessons of tolerance and compromise, on hope, on good deeds, on embracing our diversity, acknowledging our similarities, and saving lives. I was, of course, overwhelmed by the nomination. When I had time to absorb that kind of recognition, I reflected on the worldwide response to my family's tragedy and on the heartfelt goodwill that has come from political leaders and opinion makers. Apart from the fact that I can never get my girls back, it seems to me that nothing is truly impossible in this world.

Soon after the trip to Brussels, I was informed that I was to receive the 2009 Niarchos Prize for Survivorship. The prize is given by Survivor Corps, an organization that works to break cycles of victimization and violence, individual by individual, country by country. I was deeply honored to receive an award that so closely mirrors the reality of the lives of Palestinians. Nomika Zion, from Sderot, also received the award and spoke out against people who glorify war: "I am frightened that we are losing the human ability to see the other side, to feel, to be horrified and to show empathy. It's our obligation to make our leaders talk, to compel them to tell us, for a change, a different story. Maybe, one day, our voice will be heard."

I listened intently to her acceptance speech, and when I made my own, I felt I was speaking for my whole family, for all Palestinians: "I would love for a moment if my parents could come up from their grave, my wife also, and my daughters, and the Palestinian people in general and the Gazans in particular, to share with me this happy moment, and know that they are not alone . . . that someone else in this world is thinking of them. I assure you that this tragedy has strengthened me, and I am more determined than ever before to continue my efforts for the sake of humanity, but I also want you to know that willing is not enough. We must act. It is well known that all it takes for evil to survive is for good people like you to do nothing. It is time to do and to act. We have to look forward. The dignity of Palestinians equals the dignity of Israelis, and it is time to live in partnership and collaboration—there is no way backwards."

On the day of the shelling that ended my daughters' lives, we had decided as a family that we would take up the posting in Toronto that had been offered to me by Dr. Peter Singer and Dr. Abdallah Daar, and that I would come to work at the University of Toronto's Dalla Lana School of Public Health.

As we made arrangements to leave Gaza on July 21, 2009, both Israel and Hamas were seeking a truce, and Egypt was once again willing to broker it. Hamas declared that the firing of rockets into Israel from Gaza would stop, and Israel said that shipments into Gaza would start again in stages. But the rockets didn't fully stop, and the shipments remained well under expected levels.

On those summer evenings my friends and relatives gathered out on the street every night to escape the stifling heat of their houses. We sat outside my house on white plastic garden chairs arranged in two rows facing each other and exchanged the news of the day. I also carried on meeting with dozens of people who needed my help. Because I was one of the few with access to Israel and to the goods the Gazan people needed, every weekend when I came home from the hospital in Tel Aviv, I would bring filled prescriptions, shoes for a child, eyeglass lenses for one, a passport for another. I had also arranged medical appointments with specialists in Israel and ambulance transfers for those who needed them. Even the famous families, the heads of the tribes in Gaza—the Hmaid family, the Akel, the Abu Zaida—had fallen into the habit of coming to my house to discuss their health issues with me. This is my world, this is what I'll miss, and this is why our departure from Gaza will not be permanent.

There was much to do before we left in late July. Shatha studied for her final examinations day and night, holed up in the living room with the door closed, emerging only to eat, hoping to place among the top ten students in the graduating class. It was at nine thirty A.M. on the very day of our departure, July 21, that Shatha heard the official announcement of her final high school grades: 95.5 percent! Dalal was tethered to her drafting desk preparing final drawings for her architecture class. My task was to prepare travel documents for the children, find us a place to live in Toronto, get the plane tickets, and somehow pack for a five-year voyage with a family of six.

Our departure was exciting, nerve-racking, and slightly chaotic. Our extended family, friends, and neighbors had begun the good-byes the day before, gathering around us with tears, hugs, and best wishes. The six of us were filled with conflicting emotions: tears of joy combined with tears of sadness; anticipation mixed with anxiety. The younger children had never flown in an airplane or left the Gaza Strip except to come to the hospital in Tel Aviv when Shatha had been a patient there. The only planes they knew were the Israeli F-16s that flew over our home. I was concerned that the first Israeli they would see would be a soldier at the Erez Crossing, which is not in keeping with the lessons I had taught them about who Israelis are.

I took all our suitcases to the Erez Crossing early to start the inspection process, then went home and picked up the children. Once through the crossing, which took until five P.M., we were treated like celebrities. At the airport, television cameras were there to record the event, and Channel 10 TV anchorman Shlomi Eldar, who had played such a critical role in our lives, came to interview me and to say good-bye. The piece was called "The Co-Exister Has Left." He brought me a jar of sand so I wouldn't forget where I came from. Our farewell was mixed with tears of sadness and joy, of anticipation and regret. And it still took about three hours at the airport to clear the inspection for our flight, which left at midnight. As the plane took off down the runway, the children exchanged glances with me. We all knew this would be an adventure, and we were all thinking of Aya's remark, "I want to fly, Daddy."

EIGHT

Our New Home

Toronto has turned out to be everything I had hoped for: a place and a time for my children to heal. As you can imagine, I was very worried about what the transition to a new country, a new school system, new transit systems, a new language, and new friends would be like for them. Shortly after we arrived, the neighbors welcomed us to the street, and soon enough we found our way. In our first days in the new house, an incident warmed my heart. Most of the backyards around the neighborhood are fenced. The family next door has children about the same ages as my younger ones, and the first thing they did after we moved in was to take down a section of the fence so the kids could run back and forth without barriers. That simple act gave me a lot to think about. How prophetic that I witnessed what I had been dreaming about for years for our two neighbors, Israel and Palestine. Here was the manifestation of the smashing of barriers, a living example right here in my own new backyard.

Dalal and Shatha are enrolled at the University of Toronto and are doing exceptionally well, much better than even they expected. They continue to maintain a stringent study schedule and to expect nothing but the very best from themselves. In Gaza they had attended an all-girls university, but the University of Toronto is coed and very multicultural. They were among thousands of students, and in the first few days, they started to meet people of all different cultures, whereas in Gaza they were closed off from the rest of the world, there were far fewer students, students who were very much like themselves, and they knew everyone. As they work to improve themselves, they have commented that it is very different to be in a safe environment where they don't have to worry that at any moment, some event will dramatically change their lives. They see that planning for the future is possible in Canada because their plans are more likely to come to fruition. In Gaza, they were studying to have a degree and a higher education, but they knew they would never find a job in engineering. In Canada, on the other hand, they are studying engineering and know that they have a very good chance at finding work and enjoying a good career in their chosen profession. They observe that there are so many more choices even within this one profession: if one wants to study computer engineering, for example, there are many different pathways one can take; whereas in Gaza, the choices are very limited. They also say that in Canada, unlike Gaza, they don't feel that they are under someone's control; they can make their own decisions based on their personal choices.

Dalal and Shatha were both present with me during a recent interview with the Toronto radio and television station CBC. Asked to recount their very painful story, they expressed how much they miss their mother and their sisters and cousin who were killed. But they carry the message that they brought back from the Creativity for Peace camp they attended in Santa Fe, New Mexico, with Bessan. Shatha commented that before they went to the peace camp, they thought of Israelis as the enemy, but that spending time together and engaging in dialogue made any stereotypes quickly disappear. The girls they met were no different from them, and they all wanted to work together to find a solution to any conflict that exists.

Mohammed, Raffah, and Abdullah—my three youngest children—are in public schools nearby. I cannot express enough how much I appreciate the efforts of their teachers. They felt so welcomed by their teachers and fellow students that Raffah was inspired to make a speech. She felt confident enough to take the school principal by the hand and ask her to transcribe what she was saying about her experiences in Gaza. I was concerned about how my children would process the events that occurred for them in Gaza, but I can see that it is evolving in a very good way through the encouragement of the teachers and the friends we have made in Toronto. Raffah dictated her story to the principal, who wrote her words. The speech began, "Gaza is tired . . ." She continued by asking questions about how the tragedy could have have happened: "Why did Israel do this to her friend?" I could see that she had internalized what I had always tried to teach all my children: that the Israelis are our friends and we should love them as we love one another.

In a speech I made at Beth Tzedec Synagogue shortly after my arrival, an audience member asked me, "What have you personally taught your children about Jews and the Jewish people in Israel?" My answer was given by my daughter Raffah, who for the first time, along with her brothers and sisters, was attending an event at which I was speaking. I didn't know the questions in advance, and my response was unplanned. I answered the question by asking Raffah to join me at the podium and tell the audience what I taught her during the war, during the suffering. She said, "I love you" in Hebrew.

Mohammed was also encouraged to make a speech at school, and he spoke about his experiences living in Gaza. He talked about his school life in Gaza, what a typical day looked like, and what he did during the weekends. He told the story of what happened to his family, and the class reacted with much surprise, as this was something they had never heard about before. He received many letters from his classmates, each telling him how touched they were by his story and how amazed they were at his bravery. They were so open about their interest in what had happened to him and expressed their sorrow at such a tremendous loss in his life. Several letter writers mentioned how fortunate they felt to live in Toronto, and how happy they were that Mohammed was now a resident of Toronto too. Mohammed was so impressed with his classmates' kindness and by their passionate understanding; he appreciated their willingness to understand others, and he felt cared for by them. He often expresses his happiness at living in a city where he can feel free to be himself and be accepted by those around him. He has mentioned several times that he prefers to be in school and on the weekends would rather be there than at home.

Earlier in the school year, when Mohammed was still new to his school and was still getting accustomed to his new surroundings in Toronto, his class was planning to go on a trip to Ottawa, Canada's capital. He had decided not to go, as he didn't yet feel confident enough to be away from home for several nights with people he barely knew. But his classmates encouraged him to go with them, saying that their eighth grade class would not be complete without him being on the trip with them. He still talks about that unforgettable trip and is so happy his peers insisted that he was part of their school family and should be with them. School life is certainly very different here in Canada, and my children are loving all the opportunities they have there.

Abdullah is making a lot of friends, and his English is getting better and better every day. He loves his teachers and classmates and, like Mohammed, prefers to be in school instead of at home on the weekends. He enjoys playing soccer with his friends at recess and going to play at his friends' houses, where he is welcome to come over and play anytime. He seems to be growing taller every day, and he looks forward to the new clothes he can get as he grows out of his old ones. It amazed me that after only ten months in Canada, Abdullah was becoming fluent in English. His vocabulary expanded so much that when looking for the appropriate English word to say, he could think of different alternatives. During the last parent-teacher interview, I couldn't help but chuckle to myself when the teacher told me he has gone from not speaking at all to now talking too much in class. Since family discussions are very much a part of our life at home, Abdullah can debate with the best of them, toggling between English and Arabic very easily. He doesn't merely use the Arabic word when necessary, but uses it, then translates it to the English word to continue the discussion. Anyone hearing him speak cannot believe Abdullah has been in Canada such a short time.

Tragedy cannot be the end of our lives. We cannot allow it to control and defeat us. My vision for the Middle East is of a peaceful, secure, cooperative, and united place. Like Martin Luther King Jr., I too have a dream. My dream is that my children—all Palestinians and their children and our cousins, the Israelis and their children—will be safe, secure, and well fed; they will have their own citizenship and identity. This dream of mine is not going to come true with words alone. Each of us has to contribute to creating the harmony and taking an active role in promoting the dream of coexistence. Whether literate or illiterate, hungry or well fed, everyone is part of the human family. If we think collectively instead of individually, we will live as one family where we take care of one another: the stronger give more to the weaker; the wealthier give more to the poorer; the healthy help the sick; and the educated help the illiterate. *Peace* is a vague and unwieldy term in the region today. The efforts by so many to create treaties that would bring the two sides together and the continuous negotiations between countries in the region have failed to bring peace—and certainly failed to reduce the animosity, tension, and bloodshed. The so-called news from the Middle East is invariably about war starting or war stopping.

People are fed up with the lack of progress and want to find new ways to alter the insecure situations of their daily lives. For that reason, I feel we should avoid formal declarations for now. Instead, we should seek ways to be together—at soccer matches, at conferences, at family dinners. The most important step now is getting to know each other and establishing mutual respect. We share so many fundamental values: the way we socialize, the way we raise our children, the way we argue loudly and embrace ancient tradition and a sense of honor. What we need is to believe in our own ability to lift ourselves up out of this dilemma that threatens to choke all of us. We need a heavy dose of hope and optimism toward peace. My core values, which are essentially medical, tell me that people are people. If we treat each other with decency and respect, if we refuse to take sides, if we see with clarity and take responsibility for our actions, then getting past the ugliness of war is possible.

In my opinion, coexistence and cooperation, partnership and sharing at the grassroots level, is the only way forward for Palestinians and Israelis. Rather than talking about peace or forgiveness, let's talk about trust, dignity, our shared humanity, and the one hundred thousand other steps it takes to finally achieve peace and forgiveness. The conflict in the Middle East will never be resolved when there is so much hatred on both sides, when tolerance and compromise are not part of the equation. We know that military ways are futile, for both sides. We say that words are stronger than bullets, but the bullets continue to find their targets. My philosophy is simple, it's the advice parents give to children: stop quarreling with your brother and make friends—you'll both be better off.

Consider the most contentious issue: that of the right of return. The argument presented by the hard-liners in the Israeli government is that Israel is a small land and there isn't room for more people. But Palestinians can't forget the fact that Israel has plenty of room to bring Russians, Argentinians, Ethiopians, and others of the Diaspora to the Promised Land. Room is surely not the issue. Palestinians are carrying a pain that has been the burden of our ancestors; they are a nation that doesn't live on its own land and has no identity or citizenship. They are vagabonds, forced to wander from one place to another without really knowing where they are going. There is no final destination; they just keep going until they find somewhere they can settle temporarily. This is passed on from one generation to the next. It is a suffocated anger, waiting for the mercy from the heavens or for human mercy. They live in fear, frustration, and despair. All of these struggles sap their strength and make it impossible to think rationally. We must not judge Palestinians because of irrational thinking. (If you had all this on your mind, could you think rationally?) In looking for the roots of this issue, we can help them develop rational thinking, which in turn helps them and other peoples lead happier lives in community with one another.

Palestinians are in a catch-22 situation that until now has had no solution. If they accept the occupation, it means accepting all the restrictions, which are killing them: the blockades that prevent proper supplies from coming into Palestine and the lack of freedom and sheer agony of crossing the borders to travel. It is killing them to be made to feel they are insignificant, that they do not deserve a better life. They have had land taken from them that was originally theirs to live on, to grow food, to support themselves. But to not accept the situation and fight for what is theirs has resulted in many deaths too. They have been killed because of it. So, is it really a question of accepting or not accepting their lives as they are now? Does there really have to be a choice between silence or violence? In silence, you are burning with the burden of being forced to accept your lot in life; it drains your energy and makes you depressed. Violence will result in death and affect everyone.

For us Palestinians, we are waiting for something miraculous to happen, always with faith and hope, but time is passing; how is this happening in the twenty-first century? Palestinians are physically alive, but our spirits are exhausted, our patience is wearing thin, and we feel that we are not being included in this human family, that this human family doesn't care, so don't blame us if we don't listen and don't behave rationally.

Instead of silence or violence, what if we had freedom and justice? They are essential—vital—for everyone's well-being and survival. As one human family, we must give freedom and justice to every member of this family if we want to be happy, secure, and safe. If you measure happiness in your hand, it is good, but it is for you alone, but the happiness that you have by sharing it with others, imagine how much larger it would be. Happiness is for sharing, not for keeping to ourselves. We are so much better when enriched by others and much happier when there is a common joy.

* * *

Increasingly, the international community is examining the deplorable situation of Palestinians. On October 27, 2009, Amnesty International launched an in-depth report on the lack of access to adequate, safe, and clean water for the Palestinian population of the occupied Palestinian territories. The 112-page report looked at how Israeli water policies have resulted in violations of the right to an adequate standard of living for the Palestinian population, including the rights to water, food, health, work, and adequate housing.

The present standoff isn't sustainable. The people who live on the two sides know that; opinion polls say both want the situation repaired—now.

My friend Dr. Shlomo Usef thinks I should have stayed in Gaza, that in Canada maybe I'll have a rest and become a normal person. "You've never been like that," he said. "You need to come back here and finish your mission." I can assure Shlomo that I will be back and that, in the meantime, I'm fulfilling my mission from here.

Dr. Zeev Rotstein also had mixed feelings about my departure and said to a reporter:

He has a mission right now. I hope it will carry him to a productive place—a symbol of the tragedy of two peoples. Strife and hostility is completely unnecessary, unjustified. Health can be a very important bridge between the two sides. It works: you save a life, another one, do it over and over again. You don't give up. That creates an opportunity for the other side to see the face of Israelis and Palestinians rather than knowing each other only through rifles. For me, Izzeldin is a partner. He shares my vision. I want to help him in any possible way. Before this we'd been planning to establish better relations between physicians in Gaza, the West Bank, and here in Israel. We were trying to establish a learning center to improve relationships, of teaching, learning, and coordinating treatment. I think he'll come back to finish the job.

What happened to my family still strikes me as inconceivable. I lost three beautiful daughters and a wonderful, loving niece. I cannot bring them back. But I have five more children to take care of. All my children are my hope for the future, my hope for change and a peaceful world. What I can say is this: Let my daughters be the last to die. Let this tragedy open the eyes of the world. Let us ask each other, "Where are we going? What are we doing?" It's time we sat down and talked to each other. As I have said many times since the tragedy, if I could know that my daughters were the last sacrifice on the road to peace between Palestinians and Israelis, then I would accept their loss. There must be a new era, a new opportunity to think of each other with honesty. In the long years since the Oslo Accords were signed, peace talks have broken down, resumed, and then have broken down over a few square yards of proposed border—in other words, an externality. Let me tell you, there is no "magic" square yard, or hilltop, or valley, that if ceded by one side to the other will bring about peace in the Middle East. Peace can only come about after an internal shift—on both sides. What we need is respect, and the inner strength to refuse to hate. Then we will achieve peace. And my daughters will have been the last price anyone in this region has to pay.

NINE

Daughters for Life

Now you know a lot about how my daughters died, but I'd like to celebrate and honor them by telling you more about the way they lived. My daughters were special. They were modest and lovely girls, willing to reach out to those who needed help and often thinking of others before thinking of themselves. They could recite the passages in the Quran that support and highly recommend the education of all people, men and women, without discrimination. Men and Women have the right to seek education in Islam. For example,

> Narrated AbudDarda': Kathir ibn Qays said: I was sitting with AbudDarda' in the mosque of Damascus. A man came to him and said: AbudDarda', I have come to you from the town of the Apostle of Allah (peace be upon him) for a tradition that I have heard you relate from the Apostle of Allah (peace be upon him). I have come for no other purpose.
> He said: I heard the Apostle of Allah (peace be upon him) say
>
> If anyone travels on a road in search of knowledge, Allah will cause him to travel on one of the roads of Paradise. The angels will lower their wings in their great pleasure with one who seeks knowledge, the inhabitants of the heavens and the Earth and the fish in the deep waters will ask forgiveness for the learned man. The superiority of the learned man over

the devout is like that of the moon, on the night when it is full, over the rest of the stars. The learned are the heirs of the Prophets, and the Prophets leave neither dinar nor dirham, leaving only knowledge, and he who takes it takes an abundant portion.

—*Translation of Sunan Abu-Dawud, Knowledge (Kitab Al-Ilm), book 25, number 3634*

Bessan

Bessan was named after a Palestinian city, one of the oldest cities in the world, located northeast of Palestine. There is a beautiful song about the city of Bessan written and sung by a popular Lebanese singer. In the words of Debra Sugerman, leader of the Creativity for Peace camp in Santa Fe, New Mexico, which Bessan attended, Bessan was a peacemaker. Bright and beautiful, she spoke honestly and said unpopular things to speak her truths. At the camp, in the video production she was involved with called *Dear Mr. President*, she said that the girls she met at the camp had the same heart, feelings, ideas, and hopes, and that it is in collaborating with one another that they could help to find solutions to the problems in the Middle East. She said that none of the Israeli girls who were there would have wanted land to be taken from the Palestinians and that they felt badly that this had been the case.

When her brothers and sisters were asked to describe Bessan, they said that she was kind, altruistic, shy, and very wise. She blushed easily, listened much more than she spoke, and when she did speak, she extracted wisdom from her very core. She thought of others before thinking of herself, and her pocket money would most often go to buy things for her siblings: candies, chips, clothes, or any of their favorite things. She readily used to help her younger siblings with their homework in math and science, subjects at which she excelled. All of them used to ask her advice, and Mohammed especially remembers all the times she came to his defense when he was arguing with his older sisters. He also recalls how considerate Bessan was when he was not allowed to enter the premises of the all-girls university she attended, since males were not permitted. She wanted to bring her siblings to show them around and give them the tour. Abdullah was allowed because he was much younger, but Mohammed was the only one who had to stay at home. In compensation, she brought him back *shwarma*, a sandwichlike wrap of shaved meat, as a treat because she felt badly that he could not go with them.

Bessan was an example not only to her siblings but to me as well. I would often discuss issues with her and admired her wisdom, even as young as she was. I respected her opinions, and she gave me much food for thought. A few well-chosen words would stay with me, and I found myself incorporating her ideas into many of my discussions with colleagues and political leaders. She was the one who told me that everything starts small and then becomes big. Hope for a better world was always alive and well for Bessan. The memories I have of in-depth discussions with her and the level of maturity she possessed will always stay with me. My family and I—and all those she encountered—remember Bessan with awe.

Mayar

Mayar's name means "moonglow" and "one who brings goodness and beauty." Of all my children, Mayar was the one who looked the most like her mother. Mayar held fast to her convictions and had strong moral and ethical principles. Shy, quiet yet brave, she was open to the opinions and ideas of others. She was outspoken when the situation called for it; she spoke more loudly as she spoke the truth about the reality in Gaza. She had zero tolerance for injustice. She was so highly respected by her teachers and peers that she was elected president and chairperson of the student parliament in her school. She earned the trust of the teaching staff, administrators, and students of her school to the point where she was asked to assist in grading papers and examinations. She was given the key to the filing cabinet that contained information to which no other student would have been privy, and her peers were very supportive of this decision. Mayar had it all under control and was so well organized in all aspects of her home and school life. Her teachers loved her so much that they would call her at home and ask her advice. They respected her opinions and listened when she came to the defense of peers who required consideration in their particular situations.

When my children and other family members describe Mayar, they speak of someone with a strong and healthy competitive nature; someone who settled for nothing less than the very best, not only from herself but from others; someone who didn't hesitate to share opinions, but someone who listened as well as she spoke. Mayar had dreams of following my path and becoming a physician, which I look forward to seeing other strong young women make manifest.

Aya

The name Aya is popular in many areas of the world and means "phrase of the Quran" as well as as "colorful." Aya, my only child with blonde hair and green eyes, was a beautiful girl, with a great sense of humor and, true to her name, a colorful personality. She had an exceptionally close connection to her sister Mayar, who was only eleven months older than she was. They would often sleep in the same bed, share their clothes, and yet be in constant competition with each other. They might be having the most heated argument one minute, and the next they were once again attached at the hip. Aya loved to read stories to her baby brother, Abdullah. Highly competitive in every regard, Aya would always strive to be at the top of her class. When she wasn't at the top, she worked even harder to ensure that the next time, she would get the highest marks.

Generous and giving, Aya would prepare my favorite meals for me, especially when I was returning after a long absence. Aya wanted so much for me to go to her school to see what she was doing and so that I could speak to her teachers and fellow students. She was very proud of her dad and always prompted me to contribute in any way that I could. She was the happiest when I would surprise her by showing up at her school unexpectedly. Aya's deep desire to have me contribute to her school's and her fellow students' well-being often inspired me to be a better person, made me aware that there is always more we can do. Without even realizing the strong impact she had, Aya reinforced my own convictions about the need to take action and that actions are far stronger than words could ever be.

I am very grateful for all the lessons I learned from Bessan, Mayar, and Aya, and for their contributions to many people's lives, especially mine; lessons that propel me forward with more strength and determination than ever.

Daughters for Life

My daughters were full of dreams and ambitions when they were killed. But not all of the women in Palestinian society are as emancipated as my daughters, nor do they have parents or families with the resources and attitudes to support them. That needs to change.

Although compensation for their deaths was discussed at the outset, to date there has been no payment. In fact, there has been no apology. The Israeli government has taken responsibility for wrongly targeting my home and killing my daughters, but it has never apologized; no official has said, "I'm sorry." If the Israeli officials are true to their word, they will pay the compensation and apologize for the mistake they made. Then the blood of my daughters will provide the seed money to launch Daughters for Life, a foundation dedicated to changing the status and role of women.

I want an organization that will enable girls and women to speak with a stronger voice and play a more influential role in the improvement of conditions affecting the quality of life throughout the Middle East. I believe we need to accept that the women among us can contribute a great deal to the changes we need to make. Most people become exceptionally nervous when cultural change is suggested; when the status of women is challenged. But it's time to start the discussion.

Every girl in Palestine (and elsewhere for that matter) must be able to go to school. The foundation will provide scholarships for high school and university education and will examine existing programs and services to find out what's working for girls and women, and what isn't. It will develop new curriculum to fill the gaps and assist in improving current programs. At the same time, the foundation will use its funds to commission research into the advancement of girls and women and to create an advocacy program to make sure the community gets behind the changes we propose.

The ultimate objective of Daughters for Life is the creation of a credible voice throughout the Middle East on societal issues that affect the lives of girls and women. When female values are better represented through leadership at all levels of society, overall values will change and life will improve in the Gaza Strip, in Palestine as a whole, in Israel, and throughout the Middle East. That's the legacy I want to honor the memory of my daughters.

Mother for Life

You have read a lot about the details of Nadia's illness and subsequent death; you know a little about our married life together and how much I am indebted to her for her unfailing support in all my endeavors. As with the daughters I lost, I want you to know more about Nadia and the person that she was. My wife was the most dedicated wife and mother I have ever met. She was the glue that held our immediate and extended families together. Her voice of reason and spirit of unconditional generosity to those around her made her highly respected, not only by our families but also by the community at large. When she encountered a person in need and I was not around, she would do what she could to help, and she would assure the person that when I came back, she would see to it that I would do whatever I could to assist with the situation the person was in.

None of our children knew anything about kitchen chores or caring for the house. Nadia insisted that they had to focus only on school. She wanted them to be at the top, wanted them to be the absolute best they could be and not settle for second place. When our relatives asked her why the children didn't help with any of the household chores, she told them that the children's job was to study and nothing else. Nadia helped all the children with their homework every day. I really admire how she found the time for each one of the children and saw to all their needs in addition to taking care of our home. Our children went to school in shifts, and Nadia had every minute of the day timed so that when one child came home from his or her shift, the next child would be ready to begin the school day. When it came to the children's schedules, she never missed a beat.

Nadia got lots of use out of her sewing machine. It amazed me how she could tailor any piece of clothing, adjust lengths of anyone's pants or shirt sleeves, and alter the clothes of the older ones so that the younger ones could wear them. I said earlier that my daughter Mayar was the one who looked most like her mom; Dalal is the one who is most like her in her personality.

Education was so very important to Nadia. She got her diploma in the West Bank as a dental technician. When she spoke, it was obvious that she was highly educated and that even though she was a full-time mother and homemaker, she was much more than that. She could contribute to conversations in such a meaningful way that she made others take notice. Some of her most prominent characteristics were patience, forgiveness, and caring for others. She promoted and encouraged helping others and giving to charity. She was particularly sensitive to those who were poor and in need. She had so many dreams for me and for the children, and she never gave up her unconditional support of all of our dreams. She also encouraged the children never to give up. She taught them to take up the challenge and try again. She wanted them to know that there would always be another time and another chance to succeed.

I will always be indebted to Nadia for loving me and our children, and for raising our children in such a manner that I can rest assured that they had the best foundation possible during their formative years. I see Nadia's influence on them every day, and I realize how fortunate I was to have been married to such a wonderful woman. May she and my three daughters be at rest with God, and may their spirits continue to be with us always.

Epilogue

My hope for this book is that it has embraced and embodied the Palestinian people, and the tragedies we have faced, and has revealed the determination of the Palestinian people to face life's challenges and to be strengthened—not weakened—by them.

This book is also about freedom. We all must work toward freedom from disease, poverty, ignorance, oppression, and hatred. In one horrifying year, my family and I faced tragedies that mountains cannot bear. But as a Muslim with deep faith, I fully believe that what is from God is for good and what is bad is man-made and can be prevented or changed.

The first blow was the loss of my dear wife, Nadia, on September 16, 2008. The blow that does not kill will strengthen you. My children and I survived Nadia's death, becoming stronger through our need to take on additional responsibilities and to help each other survive our individual suffering.

Then in January 2009, I lost three precious daughters and a niece when an Israeli tank shelled my house in Gaza. When it is your children who have become "collateral damage" in a seemingly endless conflict, when you have seen their bodies literally torn apart and beheaded, their young lives obliterated, how do you not hate? How do you avoid rage? I vowed not to hate and avoided rage because of my strong faith as a Muslim. The Quran taught me that we must endure suffering patiently and forgive those who create the man-made injustices that cause human suffering. This does not mean that we do not act to correct those injustices.

Our great philanthropists and leaders may live to see their names written on monuments in stone or metal. But our children and the poor only write their names in the sand, and only their survivors witness those names written in stone on their graves. I want to tell what happened to my family in order to pay tribute to all the innocent people who have died due to conflicts throughout the world. Through my foundation, Daughters for Life, I hope my daughters' names will be remembered and written in stone and metal on schools, colleges, and institutions that support the education of girls. I want this book to inspire people who have lost sight of hope to take positive action to regain that hope and to have the courage to endure that sometimes long and painful journey to peace and a peaceful life. I learned from the Quran that the whole world is one human family. We were created from a man and woman and made into nations and tribes so that we may know one another and appreciate the diversity that enriches our lives. This world must embrace much more justice and honesty in order to make this a better place for all people. I hope my story will help open your mind, your heart, and your eyes to the human condition in Gaza and help you avoid making sweeping generalizations and false judgments. I hope to inspire people in this world, afflicted with violence, to work hard at saving human lives from destructive hostilities. It's time for politicians to take positive actions to build, not destroy. Leaders cannot be leaders if they are not risk takers; the risk they must take is not sending in the soldiers, but finding the moral courage to do the right thing to improve the world's human face in spite of criticism from the haters.

We must work diligently on this journey to peace. Hatred and darkness can only be driven out with love and light. Let us build a new generation, one that believes that advancing human civilization is a shared project among all peoples and that the holiest things in the universe are freedom and justice. If we want to spread peace throughout this planet, we should start in the holy lands of Palestine and Israel. Instead of building walls, let us build bridges of peace. I believe that the disease affecting our relationships—our enemy—is ignorance of one another. Judging others without knowing anything about them is what causes tension, apprehension, distrust, and prejudice. This is a big mistake. We need to be open-minded enough to want to get to know each other, and take the time to ask simple questions: What are your traditions? What do you do for a living? What can you tell me about your family? By knowing one another on a personal level, we can begin to respect each other's differences, but more important, we can begin to see how truly similar we are.

At the borders of consciousness, there is a feeling that every stranger, anyone unknown to us, is an enemy who poses a threat to us, and this impression is present in the crypts of our souls like a localized inflammation. Ask a healthy Jewish person if he or she would share a room with a Palestinian, and the answer is usually no; conversely, a healthy Palestinian is apt to shudder at the thought of sharing a room with a Jewish person. However, if they become ill and they are getting medical attention in the same hospital, it becomes acceptable to share a room with anyone, as long as their health needs are met. Illness has now become a common thread between them; they suddenly have a topic of conversation that shares the same concerns, fears, and family involvement. They may even take advice from each other and—who knows?—maybe even keep in touch afterward to see how the other is doing. I know that other common threads can be found—people don't need to be ill in order to develop supportive relationships—if only people would become more open to one another.

As a physician, I do not lose hope as long as the patient is alive. But when the patient's condition is deteriorating, I need to be willing and creative enough to search for a new course of treatment. We all need to search for the causes of our failure in the human journey to peace and discover why we are not happy, satisfied, and secure. The cause is inside us, not outside us—in our own hearts and minds. Hate is a chronic disease, and we need to heal ourselves of it and work toward a world in which we eradicate poverty and suffering. If a free society cannot help the many who are poor, it cannot save the few who are rich from hating one another.

First, we must join together to fight our mutual enemy, which is our ignorance of each other. We must smash and destroy the mental and physical barriers within each of us and between us. We must speak and move forward as one to achieve our brighter future; we are all living in one boat, and any harm to some people in this boat puts us all in danger of drowning. We must stop blaming each other and adopt the values of our, us and we.

Talking is good, but it is not enough. We must act; people are suffering and dying every day. The smallest action is more resonant and crosses more boundaries than any words. As Martin Luther King Jr. said, "Our lives begin to end the day we become silent about things that matter. In the end, we will remember not the words of our enemies, but the silence of our friends."

So what can you do? A lot. You can support justice for all by speaking out loudly to your family, friends, community, politicians, and religious leaders. You can support foundations that do good work. You can volunteer for humanitarian organizations. You can vote regressive politicians out of office. You can do many things to move the world toward greater harmony.

On March 24, 2009, in Strasbourg, France, at an exhibition called "From Hebron to Gaza," the president of the European Parliament, Hans-Gert Pöttering, referred to a visit he made to the Middle East in order to assess humanitarian needs and the rebuilding of Gaza. Here is an excerpt from his speech:

I have seen misery and lacking of the most basic food and medicine requirements, I have shared the sorrow and grief of a civilian population hurt both physically and morally. But I have also sensed hope; hope for a better future, hope for peace and reconciliation . . . The strongest indication of hope I witnessed this afternoon when I met Dr. Izzeldin Abuelaish . . . Despite the tragedy of losing three daughters, he had the strength, as a believer, as a Muslim, to continue the peace process. This is one of the strongest messages to us politicians to continue our efforts . . . After my term as president of the European Parliament, I want to use my time to continue to defend the two-states solution, a safe state of Israel and a safe state of Palestine. And if there have been human rights violations during this war in Gaza, the United Nations will have to look into it. No country is beyond international law. I think that we have to defend the truth. Sometimes, for diplomatic reasons, one does not always say the full truth—but it has to be said! We will never give up the two-state solution. And I finish with your message of hope, Dr. Abuelaish, which is a message to us politicians, to us in Europe. That what has been possible in Europe, between France and Germany, why should it not be possible in the Middle East? It seemed not to be possible after the Second World War, but we succeeded in overcoming this situation and bringing people together . . . Let us defend human dignity. All human beings are equal.

We all make mistakes and commit sins from time to time. I know that what I have lost, what was taken from me, will never come back. But as a physician and a Muslim of deep faith, I need to move forward into light, motivated by the spirits of those I have lost. I need to bring them justice.

There's a story I have been telling in my speeches that sums up the potential of one small act in the face of a situation that seems insurmountable. A man is walking along the seashore as the tide ebbs, revealing a multitude of stranded starfish. Soon he comes upon a young girl, who is picking up the starfish one by one and returning them to the sea. So he asks the girl, "What are you doing?" And she replies, "They will die if I don't get them back into the water." "But there are so many of them," the man says. "How can anything you do make a difference?" The girl picks up another starfish and carries it to the sea. "It makes a difference to this one."

I lost three wonderful daughters, but I am blessed with five other children and I have hopes for the future. I believe that Einstein was right when he said life is like riding a bicycle: to keep balanced, we must keep moving. I will keep moving, but I need you to join me in this long journey. What follows are a few of the lessons I have learned, based on my life experiences so far. I share them with you in a spirit of mutual learning.

+ Peace is humanity; peace is respect; peace is open dialogue. I don't think of peace as the absence of anything because that just puts it in a negative light. Let's be positive about what peace is—rather than what it is not.

+ The absence of war does not mean there is peace. Is a person who is ill at peace? Is a person filled with confusion and doubt at peace? Do all countries that do not engage in outright war live in peace?

+ Hate is blindness and leads to irrational thinking and behavior. It is a chronic, severe, and destructive sickness.

+ Hatred may be reversible if we allow it.

+ Anger is not the same as hate.

+ Anger can be productive. Feel the anger, acknowledge it, but let it be accompanied by change. Let it propel you toward necessary action for the betterment of yourself and others.

+ We do not need to merely accept what is happening around us. We all have the potential to be agents of change.

+ I have every faith in women and their potential. Women, by their very nature, bring people together. It is time for women to take the lead. We need to give them every opportunity to be educated and have the chance to act on what they know is best for all of humanity.

+ When your core values align with your heart, they become non-negotiable. If this is your guide, you can make decisions with the utmost integrity.

+ If you always base your judgments on truth, you will earn respect and trust.

+ To be seen by others as trustworthy is one of the greatest gifts you can receive.

+ Judging people based on another's assessment of them does not leave you open enough to consider other possibilities.

+ By exploiting others' weaknesses, you are missing the opportunity to see the great contributions they are capable of making.

+ Our children's dreams can continue to be manifested through the success of others when we put the opportunities in place for them.
+ Trust children's opinions. They are the most likely to speak the truth and far less likely to have a personal agenda.
+ Good ideas become great ones when shared with others.
+ It is not enough to sow the seeds of wisdom; we are called to action if we are to reap a bountiful harvest.
+ Whatever you do, if it is done with a sincere heart and for the betterment of others, things are more likely fall into place to make sure it happens as you envision it will.

This list will continue to grow as I keep moving through my life, picking up many more lessons along the way. I will take Einstein's advice, and I hope you will join me.

Acknowledgments

In my life I am indebted to my mother, Dalal; my father, Mohammed, my late wife, Nadia, my daughters Bessan, Dalal, Shatha, Mayar, Aya, and Raffah, and my sons Mohammed and Abdullah. I would love it if my parents, my wife, and my three lost daughters could rise from their graves to witness that the spilled blood of my three daughters was not in vain. I assure all of them that they are all remembered through me and my surviving children's good deeds and that they can rest in peace knowing that there has been much goodwill toward humanity since their deaths.

I feel privileged and thank from my heart all those who expressed compassion, sympathy, and support for my family and me in our loss: the Palestinian people, Israeli friends, colleagues, and the general public, and many members of the international community who have recognized that we must take action to stop the spread of hate. Special thanks go to Shlomi Eldar, who had the courage to expose and disclose the reality facing Palestinian civilians during the crazy war the IDF called Operation Cast Lead.

I am deeply indebted to Sally Armstrong, a distinguished Canadian journalist, who traveled to my home to meet with me and my family. Her help to me in the writing of this book was invaluable. Without that help, this book would never have seen the light.

For their enormous generosity, I would like to thank the many friends and colleagues who contributed to the creation of this book by reviewing, editing, and commenting on the manuscript, especially Anne E. Sumner, Greta Maddox, Judith Weinroth, Anne Collins, and Michael Levine.

Thanks also to Rita Mammone, a teacher and therapist in Toronto, who has embraced my family and our story and encouraged each of us to share more about our loved ones and ourselves so that the reader may help us honor and celebrate the lives of those we lost.

I would like to thank Dr. Marek Glezerman, who contributed the foreword to this book, among many other things in my life, and his wife, Tzvia; Bruno Buchet; Jean-Marc Delizée; Bertrand Delanoe, the mayor of Paris; Dr. Salam Fayyad, the prime minister of the Palestinian Authority; my Belgian friends, especially Veronique de Keyser; Luisa Morgantini, an Italian member of the European Parliament; Hans-Gert Pöttering, the former president of the European Parliament; and the Canadian government and people who welcomed my family and me with open arms.

Special thanks go to my niece Ghaida; to my lovely daughter Shatha, for her courage and determination and her ability to still be smiling; and to my daughter Dalal, who helped so enormously and has taken on such responsibility. Thanks to my brothers and sisters, aunts and uncles, cousins, and the extended Abuelaish family. Also I cannot forget the people from the Jabalia refugee camp and the people of the Gaza Strip, in particular those in the northern part, who continue to bear most of the suffering.

I would also like to thank the staff of the Kamal Edwan hospital in Gaza, the personnel who delivered the essential medical and paramedical help we received; the doctors who saved Ghaida's life and Shatha's eyes and fingers; Professor Gidhon Paret and the staff at the Sheba hospital in Israel. Special thanks to Professor Shlomo Mor-Yosef and Professor Zeev Rotstein. I am also grateful to Professors Abdallah Daar and Peter Singer, Joseph Moisseiev (the director of the Goldschleger Eye Institute), Jacqueline Swartz, Itaf Awad, Maha Daghash, Jamal Daghash, Silvia Margia, Yaacov Glickman, and Anael Harpaz.

I am deeply grateful for the support, encouragement, and wisdom of my dear friend Michael Dan. Special thanks to all I did not mention, but who I know are with me and with my children in their hearts.

A NOTE ON THE AUTHOR

Izzeldin Abuelaish, M.D., M.P.H., is a Palestinian physician and infertility expert who was born and raised in the Jabalia refugee camp in the Gaza Strip. He received a scholarship to study medicine in Cairo, Egypt, and then received a diploma from the Institute of Obstetrics and Gynecology, University of London. He completed a residency in the same discipline at Soroka hospital in Israel, followed by a subspecialty in fetal medicine in Italy and Belgium. He then undertook a master's in public health (health policy and management) at Harvard University. Before his three daughters were killed in January 2009 during the Israeli incursion into Gaza, Dr. Abuelaish worked as a senior researcher at the Gertner Institute at the Sheba hospital in Tel Aviv. He now lives with his family in Toronto, where he is an associate professor at the Dalla Lana School of Public Health at the University of Toronto. His Web site and foundation can be found at www.daughtersforlife.com.

A NOTE ON THE TYPE

The text of this book is set in Linotype Janson. The original types were cut in about 1690 by Nicholas Kis, a Hungarian working in Amsterdam. The face was misnamed after Anton Janson, a Dutchman who worked at the Ehrhardt Foundry in Leipzig, where the original Kis types were kept in the early eighteenth century. Monotype Ehrhardt is based on Janson. The original matrices survived in Germany and were acquired in 1919 by the Stempel Foundry.